the information store

Please return o
date stamped b
Con

People Like Us

Exploring cultural values and attitudes

SIMON GREENALL

MACMILLAN

Macmillan Education
Between Towns Road, Oxford OX4 3PP
A division of Macmillan Publishers Limited
Companies and representatives throughout the world

ISBN 978 0 333 97447 6

Illustrated by Lucy Truman, Brett James, Paul Hampson and Anne Cakebread
Cover design by Jackie Hill at 320 Design
Cover Photography by Haddon Davies

Author's acknowlegements
I'd like to thank:
  David Williamson and Steve Maginn for their work on the original concept of
  this project and for their continuing help and support.

  Clyde Fowle for his input and advice.

  the teachers I've met around the world during many years of seminars on
  cross-cultural training.

  Catherine Smith for her useful insights and careful editing of the series.

Acknowledgements
Interviewers and interviewees: Alessandra Crelier Azevedo, Rachel Bladon,
Charles Cho, Kazimierz Cieslak, Clyde Fowle, Dale Fuller, Hitami Hibari,
Roula Jaleb, Kylie Mackin, Steve Maginn, Uma Mani, Monika Modzelewska,
Valentina Patricola, Brandon Ruben, Jacqueline Sabri, Neeranut Samranart,
Maria Luiza Santos, Arun Sil, Oliver Thornton, Mlepe Waziri

The publishers would also like to thank Rajiv Beri, Stuart Bowie, James Boyd,
Anthony Brewer, Takashi Hata, Jeong Sook Lee, Pearl Lin, Peter Littlewood,
Tawatchai Pattarawongvisut, Cristina Roberts, Carl Robinson, Satoshi Saito,
Maria Luiza Santos, Sandra Wu, Jinsoo Yoon

The author and publishers would like to thank the following for permission to
reproduce the following photographic material:

Abode UK p10(l, m); Alamy p28(r) ©John Bower/Alamy; Art Directors and TRIP
Photo Library pp38 ©TRIP/H Rogers, 72(r) ©TRIP/A Deutsch; Cephas Picture
Library p32(tm) ©Cephas/TOP/Christine Fleurent, (tr) ©Cephas/TOP/Michel
Barberousee, (br) ©Cephas/TOP/Herve Amiard, (tr)
©Cephas/Cwphas/StockFood; Corbis pp8 ©Richard T Nowitz/Corbis, 10(r)
©Robert Landau/Corbis, 12 ©Catherine Kamow/Corbis, 16 ©Helen
Norman/Corbis, 20(m, t, bmr) ©David and Peter Turnley/Corbis, (tr) ©Ted
Streshinsky/Corbis, (mt) George Shelley/Corbis, 24(br) ©Adam Woolfitt/Corbis,
(tl) ©Yann Arthus-Bertrand/Corbis, (tr) ©Margaret Courtney/Corbis, (m)
©Corbis, (ml) ©Galen Rowell/Corbis, 25 ©Jeremy Homer/Corbis, 28(l) ©Roger
Ressmeyer/Corbis, 30 ©Ariel Skelley/Corbis, 34 ©Liu Liqun/Corbis, 37 ©Phil
Schermeister/Corbis, 38 ©Carmen Redondo/Corbis, 42(bl) ©Stephen
Frink/Corbis, (tr) ©Dallas and John Heaton/Corbis, (tm) ©Michael S
Yamashita/Corbis, 44 ©Nick Gunderson/Corbis, 46(t) ©Joel W. Rogers/Corbis,
(bl) ©Tim Wright/Corbis, (br) ©Stephanie Maze/Corbis, 48(r) ©Michael S
Yamashita/Corbis, 56(tl) ©Richard Hamilton/Corbis, (mt) ©David and Peter
Turnley/Corbis, 60(tr) ©R.W.Jones/Corbis, (l) ©Walter Rogers/Corbis, 62(l)
©Steve Chenn/Corbis, 64(tl) ©Tod Gipstein/Corbis, (tm) ©Corbis, (bl) ©Paul
Almasy/Corbis, (m) ©Peter Turnley/Corbis, 66 ©Dean Congel/Corbis, 72(l)
©Liba Taylor/Corbis; Digital Vision royalty free/Getty Images p48(l); Digital
Wisdom royalty free Mountain High Maps p4 & 5; E & E Picture Library p62(m)
©E & E Picture Library and Rav Thomas, (r) ©April Doubleday; EyeUbiquitous
p64(br) ©Paul Seheult; Format Photographers p70 ©Ulrike Preuss; Sally and
Richard Greenhill pp34(l), 50 ©Sally Greenhill; Image Bank pp8(r), 51(l);
Impact Photos pp68(br) ©Caroline Penn/Impact; Magnum Photos p14 ©Patrick
Zachmann/Magnum; PA Photos pp20(bl); Rex Features 68(t); Scotland in Focus
p42(br) ©Scotland in Focus/J Macpherson; Stone pp16, 18, 20(mr), 42(tl), 51(r),
56(tr, m), 68(tl); Telegraph Colour Library pp51(m) 60(br), 64(mr, r); Travel Ink
p13 ©Travel Ink/ray Davies.

Commissioned photography pp4, 5, 6, 7, 8(tr, mb), 11,12(b), 15, 17, 27, 29, 33,
36, 45, 49, 55, 61, 63, 64(b), 69, 71 by Haddon Davies

The author and publishers wish to thank the following who have kindly
granted permission to use copyright material:
Culture Shock! is a bestselling series of culture and etiquette guide covering
countless destinations around the world. *Culture Shock!* is published by
Times Media Private Limited, Times International Publishing Group, Singapore.
Special thanks to authors Marie-Louise Graff and JoAnn Meriwether Craig for
granting us permission to use extracts from *Culture Shock! Spain* and
Singapore respectively.

Printed and bound in Thailand

2010   2009   2008   2007
10 9 8 7 6 5 4 3

Contents

Welcome to *People Like Us*   4

1 Greetings   6

2 Name and Address   8

3 Home Comforts   10

4 Buying Food   12

5 Family Life   14

6 Dating   16

7 Personal Space   18

8 Gestures and Customs   20

9 Reflections   22

10 The Language of Clothes   24

11 Replying   26

12 Time Off   28

13 Friends   30

14 Food and Drink   32

15 Teachers and Students   34

16 Gift-giving   36

17 Complaining   38

18 Reflections   40

19 Going on Vacation   42

20 Shopping   44

21 Special Occasions   46

22 Work Customs   48

23 Weddings   50

24 Cultural Identity and Values   52

25 Face   54

26 People Like You   56

27 Reflections   58

28 Meetings and Negotiations   60

29 Holidays and Festivals   62

30 Men and Women   64

31 Table Manners   66

32 School   68

33 Homeland   70

34 Ancestors   72

35 Time   74

36 Reflections   76

Communication Activities   78

Unit Notes   82

Chatfile   93

Ben

Adriana

Chutima

Ashura

Meet *People Like Us.*

Where do you think they come from?

Brazil
Italy
Jordan
Taiwan
Thailand
India
Japan
Poland
Tanzania
The USA

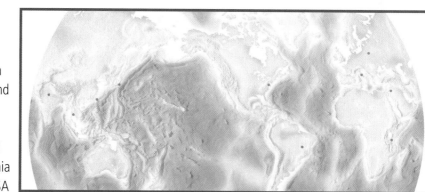

Deema

Which of these jobs do you think they do? Some people do the same job.

book publisher   businessman/woman   retired lawyer   secretary   student   teacher

How old do you think they are?

18   20   22   25   28   30   35   45   68   75

Listen and find out.

Work in pairs. Say:

– who you are
– where you come from

– how old you are
– what you do

chatfile

1

In this book, you're going to meet *People Like Us* from different countries all over the world. But remember that your culture is not just your country. It's what you do and how old you are. It's where you live. It's the things you like doing and the things you don't like doing. It's the way you talk, and your education. It's about your friends, your family, and your own character. This is your cultural identity.

You're going to use English to communicate with people from many different cultures. Cultural similarities will help you communicate more easily, but cultural differences may make communication more difficult.

This book has three aims:

• to help you find out about other cultures
• to help you find out more about your own culture
• to help you enjoy practicing your English.

Enjoy *People Like Us*

1 Greetings

Vocabulary and Listening

1 **Describe the gestures of greeting in the photos with these words.**

arm	body	bow	cheek	head	hug
kiss	lips	nod	shake	hand	shoulder	smile

Which gestures of greeting do you use in your country?

2 🔘 **Listen to four short dialogs. Match the dialog with the situation.**

a at the bank ☐   b at a friend's party ☐   c in a business meeting ☐   d in class ☐

3 **Work in pairs. Which of these expressions did you hear in 2?**

Good morning. Good afternoon. Good evening. Good day. Good night.

Hi! Hello. Pleased to meet you. How do you do? How are you?

4 **Answer the questions about the expressions in 3.**

1 Which are the most formal?
2 Which are the most informal?
3 Which do you use when you meet someone for the first time?
4 Which do you use when you know someone well?
5 Which do you use to greet other students in class?
6 Which do you use to greet your teacher?

Speaking and Listening 5 **Look at the *People Like Us* in the photos. Would you greet them all in the same way in your language?**

Valentina Patricola (Italian, student, 25)   Ben Coogan (American, student, 18)

Hiromi Morita (Japanese, student, 22)   Raj Varma (Indian, businessman, 45)

Henryk Koperski (Polish, retired, 75)

chatfile
2

Now choose an expression to greet them in English.

6 **Say which of these factors is important for you when you greet people.**

– how old they are   – how well you know them   – what they do

7 **Listen to Raj talking about greetings. Number the questions in the order he answers them.**

a How do you greet members of your family? ☐
b Are the customs the same all over your country? ☐
c How do you greet people who are important in society? ☐
d Do people greet people of the opposite sex in a different way? ☐
e How do people greet someone they've just met? ☐
f Do you hug members of your family? ☐

8 **Work in pairs and check your answers. Do you remember in detail what Raj's answers were? Now listen again and check.**

9 **Work in pairs and answer the questions about greetings in 7. Are you like the *People Like Us*?**

Name and Address

1 **Look at this envelope and answer the questions.**

1 Who is the envelope to?
2 Who is the envelope from?
3 Which is Ben Coogan's family name?
4 Which is Adriana Silva's given name?

5 What is Ben's title?
6 What street does Adriana Silva live on?
7 What is Ben Coogan's zip code?

Mr. Ben Coogan
126 River Road
Boston
MA
02108
USA

Ms. Adriana Silva
Paca da Republica 130, cj. 23
01045 - 000 Rio de Janeiro
Brazil

2 **Label the envelope with these words.**

apartment number	family name	given name	house number
state	street name	title	zip code

3 **Work in pairs. Do you write names and addresses in a similar way to the envelope in 2? Write an envelope with your name and address and label the parts.**

4 Work in pairs. Which words can you use for titles in your country?

Mr.	Mrs.	Miss	Ms.	Colonel	Prime Minister
Professor	Teacher	Director	Doctor	Engineer	

Listening and Speaking 5 Work in pairs. In these situations, which of these names do you use?

given name	family name	nickname	title

1 when you meet someone for the first time
2 with a member of your family
3 with a close friend
4 with someone you work with

6 Listen to *People Like Us* talking about what they say when they meet someone. Check (✓) the expressions you hear.

	Raj	Valentina	Henryk	Chutima
given (first) name				
family name				
title (Mr., Mrs. etc)				
nickname				

Now work in pairs and check your answers.

7 Look at these ways of choosing a child's given name.

a by choosing a grandparent's name
b by the child's race
c by the day of the week
d by consulting a fortune-teller
e by choosing a tribal name
f by consulting a priest or monk
g by choosing a parent's name

Now listen to *People Like Us* talking about the way they choose a child's given name. Match the speaker with the way of choosing.

Ben ☐ Raj ☐ Valentina ☐ Henryk ☐ James ☐ Ashura ☐ Chutima ☐

Speaking 8 Work in pairs and answer the questions.

1 How do you choose a child's given name in your family?
2 Does the given name usually go in first position?
3 Does your given name or your family name mean anything?
4 Are there given names which can be both male and female?
5 Do other people in your family have the same given name?
6 Do women change their name to their husband's name when they marry?
7 How do you know if names are boys' names, girls' names, or both?

chatfile 6

US | apartment
UK | flat

1 Work in pairs and answer the questions.

1 Do most people live in an apartment or a house in your country?

2 Which of these features would you expect to see in a typical home?

attic	balcony	bathroom	bedroom	cellar	courtyard
dining room	garage	garden	kitchen	living room	porch

3 Do the homes in the photos look like homes in your country? Say why or why not.

2 Read these descriptions of homes and match them with the photos. There is one extra description. Which house or apartment would you prefer to live in? Why?

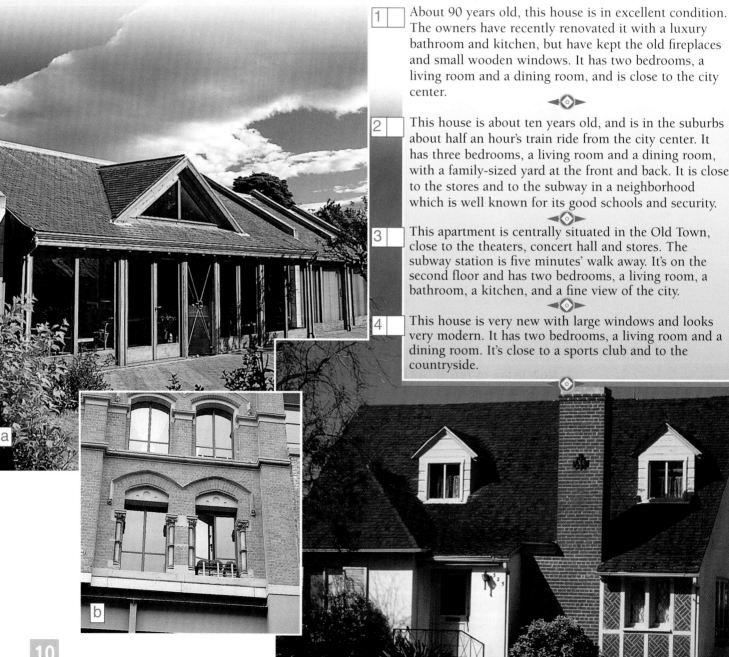

1 About 90 years old, this house is in excellent condition. The owners have recently renovated it with a luxury bathroom and kitchen, but have kept the old fireplaces and small wooden windows. It has two bedrooms, a living room and a dining room, and is close to the city center.

2 This house is about ten years old, and is in the suburbs about half an hour's train ride from the city center. It has three bedrooms, a living room and a dining room, with a family-sized yard at the front and back. It is close to the stores and to the subway in a neighborhood which is well known for its good schools and security.

3 This apartment is centrally situated in the Old Town, close to the theaters, concert hall and stores. The subway station is five minutes' walk away. It's on the second floor and has two bedrooms, a living room, a bathroom, a kitchen, and a fine view of the city.

4 This house is very new with large windows and looks very modern. It has two bedrooms, a living room and a dining room. It's close to a sports club and to the countryside.

a

b

c

Listening and Speaking 3 **Add adverbs of frequency to these statements so that they're true for your country.**

always	usually	often	sometimes	rarely	never

1 People live in apartments.
2 People prefer new homes.
3 People move several times in their lives.

4 People own their homes.
5 People share with strangers.
6 People have second homes.

4 Listen to *People Like Us* talking about homes. Which statements in 3 are they talking about? Write the number of the statements.

Chutima ☐☐   James ☐☐   Raj ☐☐☐☐   Henryk ☐☐☐☐

5 Work in pairs and check your answers. Can you remember what each person said? Now listen again and check.

Vocabulary and Listening 6 **Look at the pictures. Which of these things can you see?**

air-conditioning	bath	burglar alarm	car-parking	carpets
central heating	chair	dishwasher	drinking water	electricity
fire alarm	hot water	mattress	mosquito net	private toilet	sauna
shower	swimming pool	telephone	tennis court	tumble-dryer

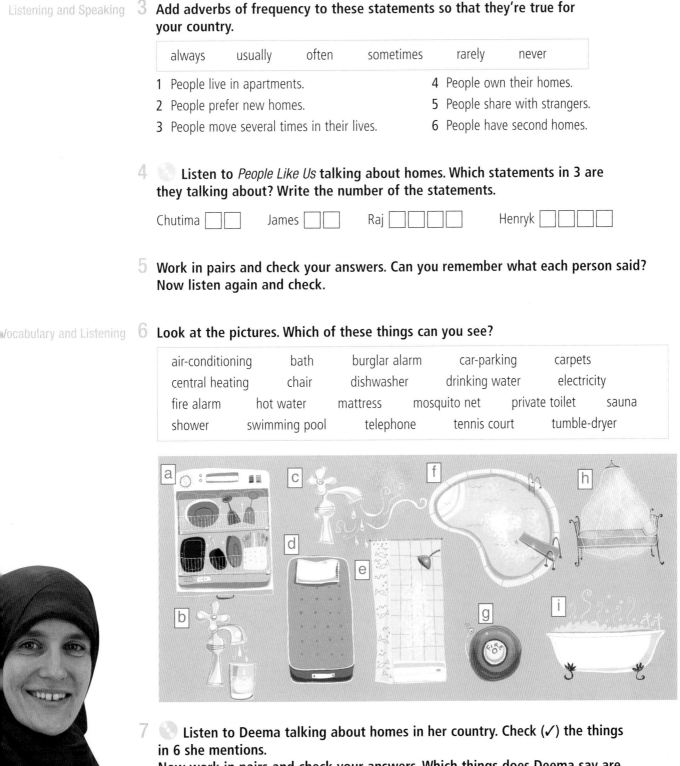

7 Listen to Deema talking about homes in her country. Check (✓) the things in 6 she mentions.
Now work in pairs and check your answers. Which things does Deema say are essential and which ones are luxuries?

chatfile
5, 6

8 Talk about homes in your country. Which of the things in 6 are usual?

11

4 Buying Food

Vocabulary **1 Work in pairs. How much do these things cost in your currency?**

> a newspaper   a packet of cigarettes   a kilo of cheese   a liter of milk
>
> a carton of orange juice   250g of butter   a kilo of fish

2 Look at the photos. Which of these food items can you see?

rice   fish   oil   beef   shrimps   chili peppers   potatoes   chicken

Reading and Listening **3 Match these questions with Chutima's answers.**

1 What items of food and drink do you usually buy every week? ☐

2 Where do you buy most of your food? ☐

3 Who does the shopping in your family? ☐

4 When do shops open? ☐

5 What time do shops close normally? ☐

6 How many days a week are shops open? ☐

7 How many times do you go shopping every week? ☐

8 What do you like about shopping in your country? ☐

9 What don't you like? ☐

Now work in pairs and check your answers.

Chutima's answers

a 'The market 5:00 a.m. Normal shops 6:00 a.m.'

b 'The local market, every day. And the shops near my place, every day as well.'

c 'I buy, once a month not every week, rice, fish sauce, cooking oil, beef, shrimps, and chili peppers.'

d 'I don't like going shopping for meat, chicken, and fish at the local market because it smells bad and it's wet. I don't like it. But I like shopping for vegetables and fruit because of the colors.'

e 'For fresh food, twice a week.'

f 'I do.'

g '10:00 p.m.'

h 'I enjoy shopping because there are many kinds of vegetables and many kinds of fruit. Sometimes I cannot eat them all, so some I put in the trash. But I still enjoy shopping.'

i 'At the supermarket and local street market.'

4 🔊 Listen and check.

5 **Work in pairs and answer the questions in 3.**

Reading and Speaking 6 **Read about shopping in Spain and answer these questions.**

1 Who does the shopping?
2 What kinds of stores are there?
3 What are the opening hours?

4 What do you bargain for?
5 Do you need to stand in line?

Shopping in Spain

There are covered markets in many towns and villages, with rows of stalls, some selling fruit and vegetables, others chicken and eggs, or meat and sausages, or cheese and dairy produce.

Each village has a street market once a week on a specific day when stalls offer a wide range of goods for sale, including food, clothes, shoes, handbags, and tourist items.

Don't bargain with the stall-holder over the price of meat and vegetables, but if you're interested in radios or watches, you might ask for a lower price.

Most big towns have an enormous supermarket, called a hypermarket, where you can buy almost anything. Here the prices are usually slightly lower than in smaller supermarkets.

The Spanish don't like standing in line, so watch out for people trying to cut in.

Market stall-holders refuse to serve people who don't stand in line and simply ignore them until they're ready to serve them.

In small towns and villages, most stores have no name or sign outside. Everyone knows what they sell and where they are.

Women do most of the shopping, although men may go to the bakery.

Women who are not working go shopping every day. It's a social occasion with separate trips to the bakery, supermarket, bank, or butcher.

Street markets start early and close soon after 1:00 p.m. Covered markets are closed during the afternoon siesta but they stay open until late in the evening, some as late as 9:00 p.m. Supermarkets open again around 4:30 p.m. Hypermarkets and department stores stay open all day.

chatfile
3, 6

7 **Talk about shopping in your country. Use the questions in 6 to help you.**

1 Work in pairs. Would you describe your family life as typical of your country? Can you use any of these words and expressions to describe your family?

single-parent family   unmarried partners   divorced   step-parents   half-brothers and sisters

2 Read about marriage and family in Algeria. Is it similar in your country?

Marriage and Family in Algeria

■ Traditionally, it was usual for three or more generations – including grandparents, married sons and their wives, and unmarried children – to share the same home. Today, in urban areas in particular, the smaller family has become more common. Mothers care for the children and household, while fathers are responsible for family income and discipline. Children don't question their parents, and they look after them when they are old.

■ Marriage is not just between two people, but two families. So parents help their children choose their marriage partners. Women generally marry in their early 20s, and men a few years later.

3 Underline anything in the text which is different in your country. Rewrite the text so that it's true for your country. Do/did you do things differently in your family?

Listening and Speaking **4** 🔵 **Listen to Deema talking about family life.**
Number the questions in the order she answers them.

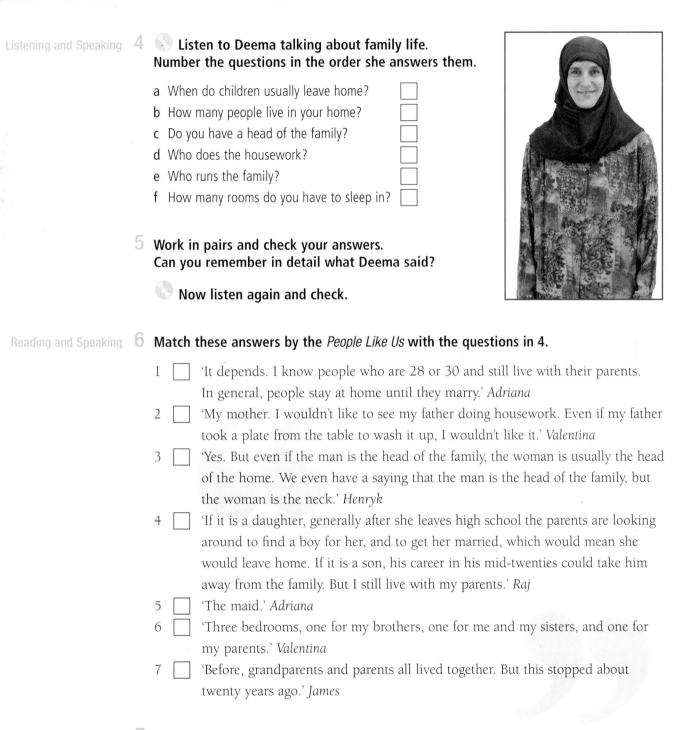

a When do children usually leave home? ☐

b How many people live in your home? ☐

c Do you have a head of the family? ☐

d Who does the housework? ☐

e Who runs the family? ☐

f How many rooms do you have to sleep in? ☐

5 **Work in pairs and check your answers.**
Can you remember in detail what Deema said?

🔵 **Now listen again and check.**

Reading and Speaking **6** **Match these answers by the** *People Like Us* **with the questions in 4.**

1 ☐ 'It depends. I know people who are 28 or 30 and still live with their parents.
In general, people stay at home until they marry.' *Adriana*

2 ☐ 'My mother. I wouldn't like to see my father doing housework. Even if my father
took a plate from the table to wash it up, I wouldn't like it.' *Valentina*

3 ☐ 'Yes. But even if the man is the head of the family, the woman is usually the head
of the home. We even have a saying that the man is the head of the family, but
the woman is the neck.' *Henryk*

4 ☐ 'If it is a daughter, generally after she leaves high school the parents are looking
around to find a boy for her, and to get her married, which would mean she
would leave home. If it is a son, his career in his mid-twenties could take him
away from the family. But I still live with my parents.' *Raj*

5 ☐ 'The maid.' *Adriana*

6 ☐ 'Three bedrooms, one for my brothers, one for me and my sisters, and one for
my parents.' *Valentina*

7 ☐ 'Before, grandparents and parents all lived together. But this stopped about
twenty years ago.' *James*

7 **Work in pairs and answer the questions in 4. Are you like the** *People Like Us***?**

chatfile
3, 6

15

6 Dating

1 **Match the expressions with their definitions.**

ask someone out	boyfriend	break up	flirt with someone	cute	ex
find someone attractive	get engaged	girlfriend	go out with someone		teenager

1 date someone regularly _____
2 like someone _____
3 handsome/pretty _____
4 invite someone on a date _____
5 a boy or man with whom you have a romantic relationship _____
6 a girl or woman with whom you have a romantic relationship _____
7 stop seeing someone _____
8 intend to marry _____
9 talk to someone in a way which shows you find them attractive _____
10 a former partner _____
11 someone who is between thirteen and nineteen years old _____

2 **Look at the photos. Which expressions in 1 can you use to describe them?**

3 **Work in pairs. Can you use any of the expressions in 1 to describe people you know?**

Reading **4** **Match Ben's comments about dating with four of these headings. Which two headings doesn't he talk about?**

a	Arranged marriages ☐	d	Age when you look for a serious partner ☐
b	Places you go to ☐	e	Parental approval ☐
c	Time to be back home ☐	f	Age when you start dating ☐

1 'It's different because I live in the city. I don't really represent the majority, I guess, because my life is just kind of unique. But, me and my friends, we just go to the park or go bowling or see a movie or go to a party or go out for something to eat.'

2 'I have friends who have serious partners, and if a couple of my friends got married to their girlfriends right now I would be surprised, but I wouldn't be shocked. But you don't go out looking for the person you're going to marry. And it's different for each person.'

3 'It depends on your parents but, I mean, when you are a young teenager you usually get home pretty early, like twelve, eleven-thirty. But then when you get to be sixteen, seventeen, you're pretty much an adult. You know as long as you show your parents you're responsible they let you stay out till when you think is appropriate.'

4 'Everyone jokes around in kindergarten and third grade, you have, like, your girlfriend. But seriously it probably starts in eighth grade, that's when you're thirteen.'

Listening and Speaking **5** **Read these statements about dating and check (✓) the ones which are true for your culture.**

	You	Henryk
1 Kids start dating at 16.		
2 They have to have an adult to accompany them.		
3 They go out to bars, parks, and to the movies.		
4 They have to be home by midnight.		
5 They start looking for a marriage partner by 20.		
6 They need their parents' approval to get married.		
7 Their parents arrange the marriage partner.		

6 🔊 **Listen to Henryk and check (✓) the statements he agrees with.**

7 **Work in pairs and check your answers.**
Can you remember in detail what Henryk said?

🔊 **Now listen again and check.**

chatfile
4, 5, 6

8 **Work in pairs. Take turns to talk about dating customs in your country. Use the statements in 5.**

7 Personal Space

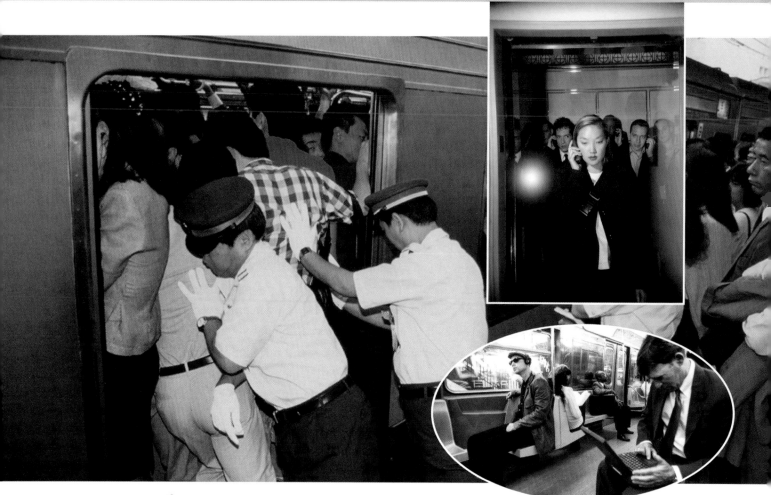

Speaking and Vocabulary 1 **Answer the questions.**

1 You're talking to a co-worker. How close do you stand?

2 You're talking to a friend. Do you touch each other?

3 Look at the diagram of a waiting room. Where do you sit when you enter?

4 You're in a crowded elevator. Where do you look?

5 You're standing in line. How close do you stand to the person in front?

6 You get on the bus. There is an empty row of seats at the back, and an empty seat close by. Where do you sit?

7 You're in a library and there's an empty seat beside you. Do you want to stop someone sitting there? If so, how?

8 You're going to the beach. Do you like to see lots of people or very few?

9 When you're talking to someone, do you look them in the eye?

10 You're on a train. Do you talk to the other passengers?

2 **Work in pairs. Imagine you are the people in the photos. Use the words to say how you feel.**

angry	anxious	cheerful	comfortable	excited	happy
nervous	OK	relaxed	stressed	uncomfortable	

I'd feel stressed.

Listening and Speaking 3 🔘 **Listen to** *People Like Us* **talking about personal space. Check (✓) the topics they're talking about.**

	Valentina	James	Hiromi
eye contact			
touching			
greeting strangers			
distance			

4 **Work in pairs and check your answers. Can you remember what each person said?**

🔘 **Now listen again and check.**

5 **Write the questions the interviewer asked.**

chatfile
4, 5

Speaking 6 **Work in pairs and play** *How does it feel?* **Student A: Turn to page 78. Student B: Turn to page 79.**

7 **Work in pairs. In activity 6, you did a role-play using aspects of behavior from different cultures. Can you guess what your partner's aspects of behavior were? How did you feel when you were doing the role-play?**

8 **Look at your partner's role-play instructions. Did you guess correctly in 7?**

Speaking and Vocabulary

1   Look at these photos. Which gestures are common in your culture? Who do you use the gestures with?

2   Work in pairs and say which part of the body you use to make these gestures.

kiss	wave	point	yawn	laugh	hug	smile	bow	kneel	hold

Listening and Speaking

3   Listen to *People Like Us* talking about some of the gestures in the photos. Check (✓) the gestures which are common in their cultures.

	Chutima	Deema	Henryk
hug			
nose rub			
hand-holding			
head to head			
body guide			
arm link			
male kiss			
bow			

4   Work in pairs and check your answers. Can you remember in detail what the *People Like Us* said about the gestures?

Now listen again and check.

Speaking and Reading 　5　**Work in pairs. Talk about any special customs you have when you enter these places.**

1 a religious building　　2 someone's home　　3 a store

6　**Read these customs. Which places in 5 are the *People Like Us* talking about? Are there similar customs in your culture?**

a ☐ 'We take off our shoes and we don't walk in, but we always walk on our knees. It's very important to take off your shoes.' *Chutima*

b ☐ 'In most households there is no custom, but in some households it is important to take off your shoes before you enter the house.' *Raj*

c ☐ 'If you are a woman, you cover your head. And if you are a man or a woman you are supposed to take off your shoes.' *Deema*

d ☐ 'There are certain rules. In Poland men take off their hat when they enter and many women cover their heads. You should also bend your knee and make the sign of the cross immediately after entering.' *Henryk*

e ☐ 'You usually have to pay respect to the Gods. We usually buy some things like some incense and oil to contribute. Usually there is an incense burner to put it in.' *James*

f ☐ 'Yes there is, you should knock first and then take off your shoes. You knock then you say 'Hodi Hodi', that's *knocking*.' *Ashura*

g ☐ 'Again another greeting. You may shake hands. The host would give this gesture of welcome, by moving their hands in a sweeping movement.' *Deema*

Speaking and Listening 　7　**Work in pairs. Do you see these gestures in your culture? If so, what do they mean?**

8 　**Work in pairs. You're going to listen to David, an expert in body language.**
Student A: Listen and find out the meanings of gestures 1, 3, 5 and 7.
Student B: Listen and find out the meanings of gestures 2, 4, 6 and 8.

Now work in pairs and check your answers.

9　**Talk about the gestures you use to mean the following:**

– hello　– beautiful　– yes　– no　– go away　– goodbye

chatfile
6, 7

Speaking and Reading **1** **Work in groups. Look at these situations and say what might be unusual.**

2 **Answer the questions. Now work in pairs and check your answers.**

1 You're traveling with a young man from the travel agency who is looking after you while you're in his country. After a while, he asks, 'Excuse me, but how old are you?' How do you react?
a You tell him how old you are.
b You pretend to be younger.
c You change the subject.
d You tell him to mind his own business.

2 When the young man from the travel agency learns how old you are, he says, 'But you look much older. And your friend is older than you, but he looks much younger!' How do you feel?
a Insulted.
b Amused.
c Flattered.
d Embarrassed.

3 You meet your new English teacher who gives you his business card. It says *Mr. Richard A. Johnson M.A. (UCLA)*. What do you call him when you speak to him?
a Richard.
b Mr. Richard.
c Mr. Johnson.
d Professor Johnson.

4 You're invited to an American friend's apartment for a meal. Where do you expect the meal to take place?
a In the kitchen.
b In the guest room.
c In the dining room.
d Anywhere in the apartment.

5 You're buying food in a market. You'd like to buy some vegetables but you think they're quite expensive. What do you do?
a Pay the full price.
b Walk away.
c Suggest a lower price.
d Buy fewer vegetables at a total price you can afford.

6 Your friend is twenty-eight, unmarried, and he still lives with his parents. What do you think?
a This is normal. It's great that he loves his parents.
b He should leave home and buy or rent an apartment.
c He should get married soon.
d It's a pity, but housing is very expensive.

3 **Choose one of the** *People Like Us* **who you think is interesting, or who you think you know well. Think about how he or she might answer the quiz.**

4 **Work in groups. Talk about how** *People Like Us* **might answer the quiz.**

Speaking **5** **Look at these topics from Units 1 – 8.**

greetings   name and address   home comforts   buying food
family life   dating   personal space   gestures and customs

Choose two or three of the topics and talk about what might be interesting or different about them when you're with people from other cultures.

1 **Look at these words for clothes. Which clothes are you wearing at the moment?**

boots	dress	jacket	jeans	shirt	shorts	skirt	socks	suit

sweater	sweatshirt	T-shirt	tie	tights	tennis shoes	trousers/pants

2 **Put the words in three groups, according to who usually wears them: *men*, *women*, or *both*.**
Now say in which of these situations you wear the clothes in 1.

at work	at home	at school	at a party	at a wedding	at a job interview

3 **Look at the photos of people wearing traditional costumes and answer the questions.**

1 Where do you think the people come from?
2 Can you describe what they are wearing?
3 Do you think they wear this costume every day or only on special occasions?
4 Do you have a traditional costume in your culture?
5 Do people wear it every day or only on special occasions?

Speaking and Reading   4   **Look at the photo of a street in India. What clothes can you see? Who is wearing traditional clothes?**

5   **Read Raj's comments about clothes customs. Are the customs similar or different to your culture?**

1   'At home you can be very casual. We have traditional Indian clothes, which men wear. Women also wear something similar, which is a long shirt and loose trousers to match it.'

2   'At school we have uniforms and at university you wear jeans and a sweatshirt.'

3   'A friend's party could be informal, so a shirt and trousers, or jeans and a shirt is fine, or it could be formal, depending on the situation.'

4   'At weddings it is very important to be formally dressed. The women wear a lot of jewelry, like bangles, necklaces, rings, and earrings. That is something that is a part of our tradition and culture.'

5   'Women have a traditional Indian dress called a *sari*, which is 8 – 10 meters of cloth which is wound around the body. This is what women wear to a wedding.'

6   'At a funeral you would wear the extended long shirt over the loose trousers and the color would be white.'

7   'Business is conducted as it is in the West, in a suit and a tie, shirt and trousers.'

6   **Write the questions the interviewer asked.**

Listening and Speaking   7      **Listen to the interview with Raj, and check your answers.**

chatfile
6, 7

8   **Work in pairs. Take turns to talk about clothes customs in your country. Use the questions you wrote in 6.**

11 Replying

1 **Look at these pictures and decide what the people are saying.**

| Sorry. | Excuse me! | Thank you. | Hello! | Hey! | Pardon me. |

You're welcome.   Come here!   Ouch!   Please.

2 **Listen and match the situations with the pictures in 1. Which expressions in 1 did you hear?**

3 **Work in pairs and answer the questions.**

What do you say ... ?
1 ... when you enter a small store where there are other people
2 ... to other passengers in a subway car
3 ... when someone sells you something and gives you your change
4 ... when someone steps on your foot
5 ... if someone holds a door open for you
6 ... when you want to attract a waiter's attention

4 **Match these comments by *People Like Us* with the situations in 3.**

a ☐ 'Well, I am a man so it doesn't happen very often for me. But, we are a very polite society and we do open the door for women and they generally say thank you.' *Raj*

b ☐ 'I would just say "Ouch!", but I would expect the person to say sorry.' *Valentina*

c ☐ '"Come here, please."' *James*

d ☐ 'Give the person a look! And if he or she apologizes, I'd just say it was OK.' *Deema*

e ☐ 'Older people usually say thank you, while younger ones just grab the money and off they go.' *Henryk*

Speaking and Listening **5 Answer the questions. Write *yes* or *no* in the *You* column.**

Do people ever say ...?	You	Ashura
1 You've put on weight!	_____	_____
2 You've lost weight!	_____	_____
3 You look great!	_____	_____
4 You look awful!	_____	_____
5 What a lovely coat! How much did it cost?	_____	_____

6 🔘 **Listen to Ashura answering the questions in 5. Write *Y* if she says yes, and *N* if she says no.**

Now work in pairs and check your answers. Can you remember in detail what Ashura said about the questions in 5? What would you say?

Speaking **7 Work in pairs. In a conversation, when someone is silent, which of these things can the silence mean?**

'I don't know.'   'I don't understand.'   'I'm thinking.'   'I don't like what you say.'
'I feel uncomfortable.'   'I'm bored.'   'I'm praying.'   'No.'

8 Look at these situations when you're with other people. Is it acceptable to say nothing?

– at a dinner party   – in a temple/church/mosque
– in a bus   – in a business meeting   – in a bar

Now think of other situations where it's OK to say nothing, and for how long.

9 Work in pairs. Read the situations below and decide if an apology is necessary. If so, who should apologize?

1 You arrive ten minutes late for your class.
2 You lose a friend's book.
3 You've arranged to meet a friend but you have to cancel.
4 You break a friend's cup or vase.
5 The sales clerk gives you the wrong change.
6 You have to leave your class early.
7 Your father forgot your birthday.
8 You arrive ten minutes late for a social arrangement with friends.

Now act out the situations.

chatfile
9, 10, 11, 12

12 Time Off

1   2

Vocabulary   **1** **Work in pairs. Look at these words for leisure activities. Which can you see in the photos?**

baseball	basketball	bowling	camping	cycling	dancing	soccer/football
gardening	going to concerts	going to the movies	golf	hiking	hunting
ice-hockey	jogging	reading	swimming	taking a bath	tennis	watching television

2 **Make a list of the leisure activities which are popular in your country. Which do you enjoy?**

Reading and Listening   **3** **Read the interview with Valentina opposite and decide where these questions go.**

a How do you like to relax personally?

b What would you say is the most popular leisure activity in your country?

c What do people do on summer and winter evenings?

d Is there any particular custom of going for a walk to a special place in the evening?

e What do people do on Friday or at the weekend?

f What is next most popular?

Interviewer	Let's talk a little a bit about leisure activities. (1) _____
Valentina	Football.
Interviewer	(2) _____
Valentina	Volleyball, then swimming, then maybe basketball.
Interviewer	(3) _____
Valentina	We watch TV all together, and in the summer we go out.
Interviewer	Would you go out every summer evening?
Valentina	Yes.
Interviewer	(4) _____
Valentina	Parents go to a movie or eat a pizza. On Saturday nights my friends and I go out to the city or a main square and meet up. There are lots of bars to have a drink and chat. Later you might go clubbing or to a private party. Afterwards we might go for a pizza or have breakfast.
Interviewer	(5) _____
Valentina	Personally, I like to do a lot of things. I used to play for the volleyball team for my town but then I quit. I used to play tennis and basketball and I quit. Then I did theater for a long time. I like performing.
Interviewer	(6) _____
Valentina	The local square.
Interviewer	How long do they spend on the square?
Valentina	Hours, walking around and talking to people.

4 🔘 **Listen and check.**

Reading and Speaking 5 **Work in groups of three. You're going to read about leisure activities in the USA, Russia, and Australia. Student A: Turn to page 78. Student B: Turn to page 79. Student C: Turn to page 80.**

6 **Complete the chart with information about the culture you read about.**

	The USA	Russia	Australia
sports			
indoor activities			
outdoor activities			
cultural activities			
weekend and vacation activities			

7 **Work in your groups and complete the chart.**

chatfile
4, 5, 6

8 **Work in pairs. Take turns to talk about time off in your country. Use the questions in 3.**

29

13 Friends

1 Match the words with their definitions.

acquaintance	boyfriend	buddy
co-worker	comrade	fair-weather friend
room mate	girlfriend	pen pal	soulmate

1 someone you work with _____
2 an informal word for a friend _____
3 someone you don't know very well _____
4 someone you write to _____
5 someone who lives in the same apartment as you _____
6 someone who shares the same view of life as you _____
7 someone who is only a friend during the good times _____
8 someone who has the same socialist beliefs as you _____
9 someone you have a romantic relationship with _____ _____

Can you think of names of people you know who you can describe using these words?

2 Work in pairs and answer these questions about you and your friends.

1 Where and when did you meet them?
2 How often do you see them?
3 Do you ever all go out together?
4 How much do you know about them?
5 Do you often make new friends?

3 Read the questionnaire and check (✓) the statements you agree with.

WHAT WOULD YOU EXPECT A GOOD FRIEND TO DO FOR YOU?

		You	Your partner
1	lend you a small amount of money		
2	lend you a lot of money		
3	lend you clothes		
4	give you a room in their home		
5	listen to your problems		
6	help solve your problems		
7	give you advice		
8	use their influence to help you		
9	agree with you all the time		
10	tell you when you're wrong		
11	put business second and you first		
12	put their family second and you first		
13	lie to protect you		
14	make no other friends		
15	see you often		
16	be available to talk or meet at all times of the day		

4 Work in pairs. Take turns to ask each other about what you would expect a good friend to do for you. Check (✓) the *Your partner* column in the chart.

Reading and Listening 5 Work in pairs. Read the situations and talk about what you think went wrong.

1 On vacation in the UK, Raoul was sitting on a park bench when a man sat down beside him. The man nodded his head and smiled, but he didn't say anything. Raoul was embarrassed and felt that English people are always very cold and distant. Was his reaction fair?

3 Tony invited Indira to visit his home one day. They spent a few minutes chatting but then the phone rang and Tony spent half an hour talking to his friend on the phone. Indira was upset and left. Was she right to feel so angry?

2 Michiko was working as a secretary in Sydney and made friends with Judy. They often had lunch together, and Judy helped Michiko sort out problems with settling in to live in Australia. They saw each other most days or talked on the phone, but Michiko didn't invite Judy home because she shared her apartment with three other people. After a while, Judy started to see less of Michiko and started having lunch alone. Michiko began to feel Judy was avoiding her. What do you think was the problem?

6 🔵 Listen to Barbara, an expert in cross-cultural communication, talking about what went wrong in the situations in 5. Did you guess correctly? Does Barbara suggest what the people should do next time this happens?

chatfile
3, 14

Speaking 7 Work in pairs. Choose a situation in 5. Think about what the people did next time this happened. Act out the situation.

14 Food and Drink

borscht, Russia

tagine, Morocco

sushi, Japan

mezes, Turkey

Vocabulary and Speaking

1 Match these traditional dishes from around the world with the photos.

a lamb or chicken and vegetables _____

b small portions of eggplant, _____
   stuffed peppers, beans, for example

c beetroot and cabbage soup _____

d raw fish, rice, and seaweed _____

Have you ever tried any of these dishes?

US | chips
UK | crisps

2 Work in pairs. Which of these items of food are traditional in your country? What other food is traditional in your country?

caviar   chips   hamburger   pasta   pizza   salad   sandwich   spare ribs   steak

Reading and Listening

3 Work in pairs and answer the questions.

a Is it acceptable to eat in the street?

b How long does a typical meal last?

c What kind of food do you eat when you have guests for dinner?

d If you had a special guest for dinner and you wanted to impress them, what would you offer them?

e What do people eat with: knife, fork, spoon, chopsticks, or their hands?

f How many meals a day do people have and at what times?

4 **Read the interview with Ben and decide where the questions in 3 go.**

Interviewer	(1) _____
Ben	Teenagers probably have four. Yeah, eat some breakfast, eat lunch at school, get out of school and have a slice of pizza, go home and have dinner.
Interviewer	So, after school you have a slice of pizza?
Ben	Or chips or something.
Interviewer	And what time will you have those meals?
Ben	Breakfast 7:30, then lunch 12:00, then 3:30 or 4:00, and dinner 7:00.
Interviewer	(2) _____
Ben	Breakfast, ten to fifteen minutes, if that. Lunch, thirty minutes. The meal after school, you probably eat it on your way home, so you don't even really stop for that. And dinner, probably forty-five minutes.
Interviewer	(3) _____
Ben	Knife and fork. If you eat Chinese food, chopsticks, and if you're eating a sandwich, your hands.
Interviewer	(4) _____
Ben	Yeah. Depends what you're eating. If you have something really messy like ribs with rice or something, people will look at you. But if you're walking along eating a sandwich no one cares.
Interviewer	(5) _____
Ben	If it's good friends you eat whatever, you know – barbecue, hamburgers, or cold Chinese. But if it's people that you're just getting acquainted with, then you want to have good food, like some steaks or some nice pasta with some salad.
Interviewer	(6) _____
Ben	Steak, I guess. Or, if you really want to impress them – caviar!

5 **Listen and check.**

6 **Work in pairs. Listen to Hiromi and Valentina talking about food. Which questions in 3 are they answering? Write the letter (a-f) of the questions.**

Hiromi ☐ ☐ ☐   Valentina ☐ ☐ ☐

7 **Work in pairs and discuss Hiromi and Valentina's answers. Can you remember in detail what they said?**

Now listen again and check.

Speaking 8 **Work in pairs. Take turns to think of a typical dish in your country and describe it to your partner. Don't say what it is. Your partner must guess the dish you're describing.**

chatfile
3, 6, 15

33

15 Teachers and Students

Vocabulary and Speaking

1 **Look at the photos. Does either look like a typical class in your country?**

2 **Work in pairs. Which of these features do you expect to see in a typical classroom?**

blackboard	bookshelves	chairs	computer	desks	newspapers
overhead projector	posters	maps	tables	textbooks	video player	whiteboard

Which features can you see in the photos?

3 **Work in pairs and draw a typical classroom in your country. Say where things are.**

Reading and Speaking

4 **Read these statements and say which are true for your country.**

1 The students stand up when the teacher comes into class.
2 The students call their teacher *Sir* or *Madam*.
3 The teacher speaks most in the class.
4 The students are encouraged to ask questions and give their opinions.
5 The teacher only follows the textbook.
6 The textbook has more authority than the teacher.
7 The teacher always has to know the right answer.
8 The students often work in groups.
9 The students sit at desks facing the teacher at the front of the classroom.
10 The students often cheat during exams.

5 **Match these comments by** *People Like Us* **with the statements in 4.**

a ☐ 'Sometimes by their first names, but normally *teacher*.' *Adriana*

b ☐ 'Yes, a teacher is expected to do their homework better than the students.' *Raj*

c ☐ 'This is the door, and here is a stage and on the stage there is the table for the teacher and then we have our desks, which are for two people, in three rows.' *Valentina*

d ☐ 'Yes, they are, but usually students don't express their opinions. The teachers sometimes don't ask for students' opinions, as they might not be what the teachers think.' *Valentina*

e ☐ 'Absolutely not, each student is expected to answer his or her own questions without looking at anyone else's paper.' *Raj*

f ☐ 'There are about four rows of desks and about ten seats back.' *Hiromi*

g ☐ 'I think there's an exchange of ideas. The teacher says something, the students elaborate. There are some teachers who are stricter and tend to monopolize the class time.' *Adriana*

h ☐ 'I tell my students that I am not sure if my answer is right, so I will go and check and I will tell them tomorrow.' *Chutima*

i ☐ 'It depends on the personality of the teacher. Small children believe what their teachers say. In secondary schools students who want to know more look things up in different sources and compare the sources. The teacher is not the authority for them any longer.' *Henryk*

j ☐ 'They call the teacher by name, like *Teacher Oliver*, something like that. They don't call them *Madam* or *Sir*.' *Ashura*

k ☐ 'They follow the coursebook, but they also add their own ideas.' *Chutima*

Speaking and Listening **6** **Work in pairs. Look at this list of typical activities in English lessons. Decide if they are serious (✓), not serious (✗), or put (?) if you don't know.**

a pair work ☐   d correction ☐   g pronunciation ☐   j listening ☐
b songs ☐   e speaking ☐   h dictionary work ☐   k writing ☐
c games ☐   f grammar rules ☐   i translation ☐   l role-plays ☐

7 🔘 **Listen to Jenny, an experienced teacher of English, talking about the activities in 6. Check (✓) the items she mentions. Which does she think are most important?**

chatfile
4, 5, 6, 19

8 **Work in pairs and check your answers. Can you remember why Jenny thinks the activities are important? Do you agree with her?**

16 Gift-giving

1 **Work in pairs. Which of the following are suitable gifts in your culture?**

baseball cap	bottle of perfume	bottle of whisky	bottle of wine
box of chocolates	cake	calendar	clock	handkerchief	money
pair of jeans	pair of scissors	pen	toy	underwear

Which items can you see in the photos?

2 **On which of these occasions do you give gifts?**

New Year   Christmas   someone's birthday   mid-summer   mid-winter   a dinner party
a cocktail party   a house-warming party   a wedding   a name day   a funeral

Can you think of other occasions when you give gifts? What do you give?

3 **Listen to Chutima talking about gift-giving. Number the questions in the order she answers them.**

a What about a religious holiday? ☐

b Do people open a gift immediately? ☐

c When do people give gifts in Thailand? ☐

d Are there any things which are unsuitable presents? ☐

e If you go to someone's party, if you take something to eat or drink, do you expect the host or hostess to share it with you during the dinner? ☐

f What sort of gifts do people take for a dinner party or a birthday party? ☐

g Which hand do you use to give a gift? ☐

h What do you give at a wedding? ☐

4 **Work in pairs and check your answers. Do you remember in detail what Chutima's answers were?**

Now listen again and check.

5 **Work in pairs and answer the questions in 3.**

Reading and Speaking 6 **Read the text, which gives advice for visitors to China. Which paragraph describes what you can see in the photo?**

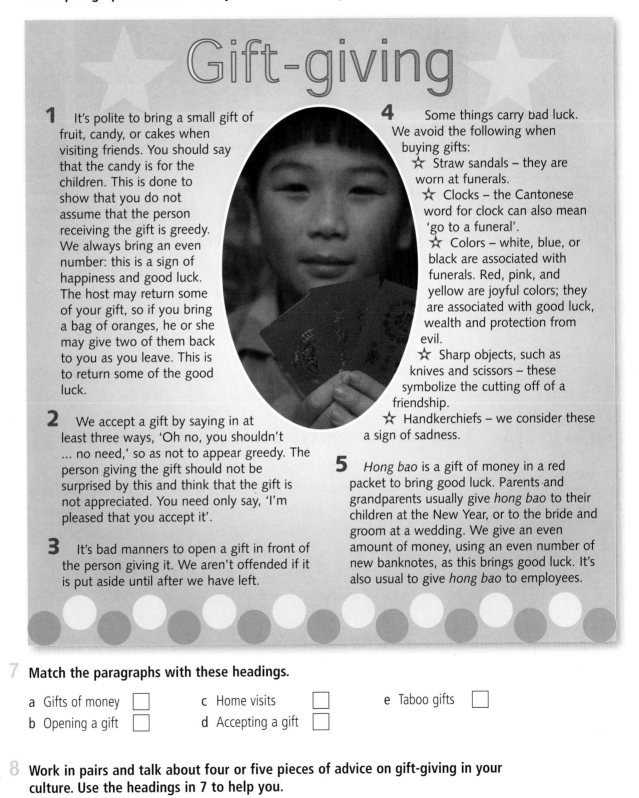

Gift-giving

1 It's polite to bring a small gift of fruit, candy, or cakes when visiting friends. You should say that the candy is for the children. This is done to show that you do not assume that the person receiving the gift is greedy. We always bring an even number: this is a sign of happiness and good luck. The host may return some of your gift, so if you bring a bag of oranges, he or she may give two of them back to you as you leave. This is to return some of the good luck.

2 We accept a gift by saying in at least three ways, 'Oh no, you shouldn't ... no need,' so as not to appear greedy. The person giving the gift should not be surprised by this and think that the gift is not appreciated. You need only say, 'I'm pleased that you accept it'.

3 It's bad manners to open a gift in front of the person giving it. We aren't offended if it is put aside until after we have left.

4 Some things carry bad luck. We avoid the following when buying gifts:
☆ Straw sandals – they are worn at funerals.
☆ Clocks – the Cantonese word for clock can also mean 'go to a funeral'.
☆ Colors – white, blue, or black are associated with funerals. Red, pink, and yellow are joyful colors; they are associated with good luck, wealth and protection from evil.
☆ Sharp objects, such as knives and scissors – these symbolize the cutting off of a friendship.
☆ Handkerchiefs – we consider these a sign of sadness.

5 *Hong bao* is a gift of money in a red packet to bring good luck. Parents and grandparents usually give *hong bao* to their children at the New Year, or to the bride and groom at a wedding. We give an even amount of money, using an even number of new banknotes, as this brings good luck. It's also usual to give *hong bao* to employees.

7 **Match the paragraphs with these headings.**

a Gifts of money ☐   c Home visits ☐   e Taboo gifts ☐
b Opening a gift ☐   d Accepting a gift ☐

chatfile
4, 5, 6, 16

8 **Work in pairs and talk about four or five pieces of advice on gift-giving in your culture. Use the headings in 7 to help you.**

Speaking and Listening

1 **Look at the photos. Where is it? Who is the man? What do you think the woman is doing?**

2 **Listen and check.**

Reading and Speaking

3 **Work in pairs. Read these situations and talk about how you would react.**

1 You're waiting to be served in a restaurant. How long would you expect to wait before your food arrived? What would you do or say if you waited much longer?

2 The sales clerk is dealing with your request, and then the telephone rings. She turns away and spends ten minutes on the phone. What would you do or say?

3 The bus driver is driving too fast. What would you do or say?

4 The waiter in a restaurant has made a mistake with your bill and has charged you too much. What would you do or say?

4 **Match these comments by *People Like Us* to one of the situations in 3.**

a ☐ 'If you are uncomfortable and find that he is breaking speed limits, you would speak to the conductor and tell him to ask the driver to slow down.' *Raj*

b ☐ 'If I've ordered a restaurant's speciality, I expect to be served soon. I could wait longer for more sophisticated dishes. If it's too long, however, I would just leave. I would go somewhere else.' *Henryk*

c ☐ 'I would tell him to reduce his speed, and if he still drove too fast I would jump off the bus.' *Ashura*

d ☐ 'It would depend. If you find that the assistant is talking to a friend and is ignoring you, you would probably walk away and go to another shop. However, if you find that the assistant is dealing with another customer and asks you to wait, you would probably wait till she or he finishes.' *Raj*

e ☐ 'I would point it out to him. If he were impolite I would call the manager of the restaurant.' *Henryk*

f ☐ 'It depends on the food ordered, but mostly I would wait for the food for 15 - 30 minutes. And if the food was taking longer, I would go and ask, "Why is the food taking so long?"' *Ashura*

g ☐ 'I would take back all the goods that I want to buy and walk out.' *Chutima*

5   Work in pairs. Would you react in the same way as the *People Like Us*?

Speaking   6   Look at these situations. Can you imagine what the customer's complaint is?

7   Work in pairs and choose a situation in 6. Act out the dialog.

chatfile
11, 12, 13

39

Speaking and Reading **1 Work in groups. Look at these situations and say what might be unusual.**

2 Answer the questions. Now work in pairs and check your answers.

1 You're waiting to be served in a store. Another customer walks in. What you do expect to happen?
a The customer says 'good morning' and the other customers don't reply.
b The customer says 'good morning' and everyone replies.
c The sales clerk says 'good morning' and the customer replies.
d Nobody says anything.

2 Your friend has invited you for dinner, but you haven't finished your homework by the time you need to leave. You need to give it to your teacher tomorrow morning. What do you do?
a Telephone your friend and apologize for not being able to go.
b Stay at home and don't phone your friend. Your friend will understand.
c Go to your friend's home and do your homework when you get back.
d Telephone your friend and pretend you're ill.

3 You don't understand something your teacher says, and would like an explanation. What do you do?
a Interrupt the teacher and ask for an explanation.
b Nothing.
c Wait until the end of the class and ask for an explanation.
d Raise your hand, wait for the teacher to notice you, and then ask for an explanation.

4 You're in a restaurant and your waiter brings you the wrong food. What do you do?
a Ask to speak to the manager.
b Explain to the waiter that he has brought the wrong food.
c Say nothing and eat the food you haven't ordered.
d Complain loudly and ask the waiter to bring the correct food.

5 A friend visits you at home and brings you a gift. As she gives it to you, what do you say?
a 'Oh, you shouldn't have!'
b 'Thank you very much.'
c 'I'm not worthy of receiving a gift from you.'
d 'What is it?'

6 You're having breakfast at a friend's home. What might there be to eat?
a Noodles.
b Steak and eggs.
c Cornflakes.
d Something else.

3 Choose one of the *People Like Us* who you think is interesting, or who you think you know well. Think about how he or she might answer the quiz.

4 Work in groups. Talk about how *People Like Us* might answer the quiz.

Speaking **5** Look at these topics from Units 10 – 17.

the language of clothes   replying   time off   friends   food and drink
teachers and students   gift-giving   complaining

Choose two or three of the topics and talk about what might be interesting or different about them when you're with people from other cultures.

THAILAND

HONG

Maldives Cruise

scotland

Speaking and Vocabulary

US	vacation
UK	holiday

1 Work in pairs. Look at these adverts for vacations. Which vacation would you like to go on?

2 Say which of these activities you can do on each vacation.

fishing	lying on the beach	playing golf	sightseeing	snorkeling
swimming	visiting cities	visiting old buildings	walking	

3 **Work in pairs and answer the questions.**

1 What do you like doing when you go on vacation?

2 What are the most popular tourist destinations for visitors to your country?

3 What can visitors do and see in your country?

4 **Think about your answers to these questions.**

1 Do people take long vacations (two weeks or more) or short vacations (one week or less)?

2 Where do most people like to go?

3 What's the best time to come to your country? Why?

4 What would your ideal vacation be? Where would you go?

5   Listen to *People Like Us* talking about going on vacation. Which questions in 4 are they answering? Write the number of the questions.

Henryk   ☐ ☐ ☐

Raj   ☐ ☐ ☐

Ashura   ☐ ☐

Ben   ☐

Chutima   ☐ ☐

Adriana   ☐

Valentina   ☐

6 **Work in pairs and check your answers. Which answers are most similar and most different to your answers?**

  Now listen again and check.

Speaking 7 **Read these statements about travel. Do you agree with them?**

   " The trouble with vacations is that I never want to come back! "

   " What's the point in traveling abroad? I have everything I need here at home. "

chatfile
3, 4, 5, 14

8 **Work in pairs and answer these questions.**

1 What five things do you miss when you're away from home?

2 What five things do you like when you go on vacation to another country?

20 Shopping

Vocabulary and Speaking

1 Work in pairs. Look at the photo of a shopping mall. Do you have shopping malls like this in your country? Which of these places and shops do you find there?

bookstore	clothes' store
department store	drugstore
electrical hardware store	
household store	jeweler
movie theater	record store
restaurant	sports' store

2 Work in pairs. Say which places and stores in 1 you would visit to buy these things.

an *Omega* watch	a *Harry Potter* book
Chanel perfume	a pair of *Nike* tennis shoes
a necklace	a *Robbie Williams* CD
dinner plates	a palmtop computer
a *Four Seasons* pizza	

3 Look at these items *People Like Us* buy when they go shopping at home or in another country. Check you know what they mean. Which of these things do you buy when you're away from home?

chocolate	clothes	cosmetics
food	hats	jewelry	key rings
pictures	souvenirs	toys

44

Reading and Listening 4 **Match these questions with Ben's answers.**

1 Do you enjoy shopping for gifts for others, and for yourself? ☐

2 How often do you buy clothes for yourself? ☐

3 How much do you spend on clothes in a year? ☐

4 Do you ever go shopping but buy nothing? ☐

5 If you go to another country, do you usually buy souvenirs? ☐

6 What do you do in shopping malls, apart from shopping? ☐

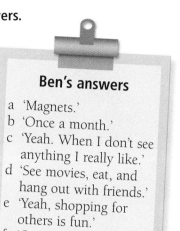

Ben's answers

a 'Magnets.'
b 'Once a month.'
c 'Yeah. When I don't see anything I really like.'
d 'See movies, eat, and hang out with friends.'
e 'Yeah, shopping for others is fun.'
f 'Over a thousand dollars.'

5 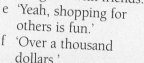 **Listen and check. Is there anything that Ben said that surprises you?**

6 **Match these comments by *People Like Us* with the questions in 4.**

a ☐ 'I usually don't buy much for myself or others, but at the moment I'm going through a phase of renovating my wardrobe and I'm spending lots.' *Adriana*

b ☐ 'I don't enjoy shopping for myself. I leave buying gifts for other people to my wife. In my opinion women have better intuition.' *Henryk*

c ☐ 'No, I don't enjoy shopping for gifts for myself or others. I personally believe in buying what is absolutely necessary, and that is not a gift. However, a lot of people enjoy shopping for gifts both for themselves and others.' *Raj*

d ☐ 'Yes, sometimes I go but don't see anything interesting or anything I like. I just go window-shopping and then I come back.' *Ashura*

e ☐ 'Key rings, I always buy key rings and chocolate.' *Chutima*

f ☐ 'I am not sure, it depends on how many parties I have! If I buy a Thai suit it's quite expensive, both for the material and for making to order. Sometimes I buy the material and then the dressmaker makes it, so maybe 10,000 baht I think. Recently I bought a dress, a shirt, T-shirt, shoes, jeans.' *Chutima*

g ☐ 'People walk around and do some window-shopping. You could go to MacDonald's and have a coffee, you could go to a video bar and play video games or to a music shop and listen to music.' *Raj*

Speaking 7 **Work in pairs and answer the questions in 4. Are you like the *People Like Us*?**

chatfile
3, 6

21 Special Occasions

Vocabulary and Reading

1 **Look at the photos and say which of these special times and occasions you can see.**

adolescence	anniversary	birth	special birthday
death	Eid	marriage	name-giving	retirement

2 **Look at some expressions you can use on special occasions. When do you use them?**

Happy Birthday! Congratulations! I'm so sorry to hear the news. Welcome!

Your good health! Best of luck! Cheers. Have a wonderful time. Deepest sympathies.

46

3 **Read the text about two special occasions in Thailand.**
Find out when they happen, what happens, and why they happen.

When the newborn baby is a month old, the parents give a feast for relatives and friends, and the baby has its first haircut. This ceremony protects the baby from evil spirits who like to make themselves at home in the hair. It announces to the world that the baby has been born, has survived the most dangerous period of its life and is ready to be introduced into the Buddhist community.

Thais consider every 12th birthday of life particularly important and usually celebrate it with a special party at the house and by inviting nine monks to chant. Gifts of money from visitors are especially appreciated if the amount is 9 or 99, or even 999 baht. Most important is the 60th birthday, which often marks retirement from the active world. ■

Speaking and Listening **4** **Work in pairs and make a list of special occasions in your country.**

5 ⬤ **Listen to** *People Like Us* **talking about special occasions. Which special occasions in 1 are they talking about?**

Ben _____   Henryk _____

Raj _____   Chutima _____ _____

Valentina _____

6 ⬤ **Listen again and answer the questions.**

1 What special birthdays are there in the USA?

2 Who chooses the child's given name in India?

3 How long do people visit after a funeral in Italy?

4 What is the 50th wedding anniversary called in Poland?

5 Why do you think Chutima says a funeral in Thailand is quite expensive?

6 Why does Chutima release turtles on her birthday?

Speaking **7** **Work in pairs. Choose one of these topics and answer the questions about special occasions in your country.**

chatfile
6, 18

1 **A typical birthday**
What do people usually do?
Who do they celebrate with?
What kind of presents do they get?
What other things do they do?

2 **A special tradition or custom**
What time of year is it?
How do you celebrate?
What is the reason for the tradition or custom?
Is it the same now as it was in the past?

1 **Work in pairs. Look at the photos and answer the questions.**

1 Which work situation are you likely to see in your country?
2 Which work situation would you like to work in?

2 **Work in pairs. What qualities do you think are necessary to do these jobs?**

accountant	computer programer	driver	firefighter	journalist
police officer	receptionist	sales representative	teacher	

You can use these words to help you.

fashionable	fit	funny	hard-working	imaginative	intelligent
kind	lively	organized	practical	reliable	smart	sociable

To be an accountant you need to be hard-working.

3 **Work in pairs. Take turns to explain what these words and expressions mean, and what advantages they bring to a job.**

a medical care
b bonuses
c opportunities for travel
d housing
e a retirement fund

f recreation facilities
g a cafeteria
h a company car
i job security

j a good salary
k long vacations
l flexible working hours
m transportation allowance

4 Work in pairs. If you're looking for a job in a company, what features in 3 are important to you? Choose six features and mark them 1 (most important) to 6 (least important).

5 Work in pairs and choose two jobs from 2. If an employer wants to employ someone to do these jobs, which of these things is he or she looking for?

good qualifications	political record	variety of experience in different jobs
initiative	self-confidence	ability to work in a team	gender
independence	ability to cope in a crisis	

Reading and Listening

6 Work in pairs. Read these statements about work customs in the USA. Check (✓) the statements which are true for your country and put (?) next to any you don't agree with or are not sure are true.

	Your country	Adriana	James
1 Typical working hours are 9 to 5.			
2 If we work in an office we wear neat clothes, and men wear a suit and a tie.			
3 We have an hour for meal breaks.			
4 Most people expect to work late sometimes.			
5 We usually have two to three weeks vacation a year.			
6 Men usually retire at 65 and women at 60.			
7 We get paid at the beginning and in the middle of the month.			
8 Some people get perks, such as a company car or a retirement plan.			
9 Some people get bonuses.			
10 Women have the same opportunities as men.			
11 Most people change their jobs several times in their working lives.			
12 Co-workers are often friends.			
13 We often use personal connections to get work for relatives.			

chatfile
6

7 Listen to Adriana and James and check (✓) the statements they agree with. Put (?) if you don't know, or if they don't talk about a statement.

Speaking 8 Work in pairs and talk about the statements in 6. Are you like the *People Like Us*?

Vocabulary and Reading **1** **Describe the photo of a traditional wedding ceremony in Britain. Use some of these words.**

best man	bride	bridegroom	bride's father
bridesmaid	church	guests	minister

2 **Read the description of the stages of a traditional wedding in Britain. Number them in the correct order. The first stage is in the correct position.**

1 Weddings in Britain can take place in either a church or a registry office, although there are some other places which have a license for weddings. Weddings usually take place on a Saturday.

☐ After the meal, there may be music and dancing. Then the bride and groom say goodbye to everyone before they go away on their honeymoon. As the bride leaves she throws her flowers for her friends to catch. The woman who catches the flowers will be the next to marry!

☐ As the newly married couple come out of the church, the guests throw confetti or rice. Then everyone takes photos.

☐ Traditionally the bride arrives a few minutes late at the church with her father, or the person who is 'giving her away', who accompanies her to the altar where the minister is waiting.

☐ The ceremony begins. The couple take their wedding vows and they exchange rings. They sign the wedding certificate and they leave the church. It all takes about an hour.

☐ In a traditional wedding, the families and the other guests arrive at the church in good time. The groom's family sits on the right and the bride's family on the left.

☐ After the ceremony, everyone goes to the reception. The bride's father, the best man, and the groom all make speeches, and everyone toasts the happy couple. The bride and groom cut the wedding cake. Guests send presents before the wedding or bring them to the reception. Gifts of money are not usual.

☐ The night before the wedding, there's a tradition that the bride and groom should not see each other, and the groom is not meant to see the bride's dress until the day of the wedding. The wedding dress is traditionally white.

3 **Read these statements about weddings in Britain. Are they true (T) or false (F)?**

1 You can have either a religious ceremony in church or a civil ceremony in a registry office.
2 The traditional color for the bride's dress is red.
3 The bride arrives on time at the church.
4 Only relatives are invited to the wedding.
5 The bride arrives on her own.
6 The bride doesn't usually make a speech at the reception.
7 The bride and groom leave before the end of the reception.

4 **Look at these photos of a traditional wedding in Britain. Which stages can you see?**

Listening and Speaking 5 Work in groups of three. You're going to hear Chutima and Deema talking about a traditional wedding.
Student A: Turn to page 78. Student B: Turn to page 79. Student C: Turn to page 80.

6 **Work in your groups and complete the chart.**

	Chutima	Deema
Special customs and traditions		
Before the ceremony		
During the ceremony		
After the ceremony		
Typical gifts		

7 Listen again and check.

chatfile
6

8 **Describe a wedding you've been to in your country or another country. Use the description in 2 and the chart in 6 to help you.**

51

1 **Write down words which you associate with these things. Use the pictures to help you.**

childhood	family	home	money
neighborhood	politics	religion	school

Now work in pairs and discuss your words.

2 **Listen to Robert, who is English, talking about his cultural identity and values. Check (✓) the words he associates with the things in 1.**

bad	church	corrupt	criminal	duty	good	helpful	hope
laughter	liar	opportunity	oppression	patriotism	power	priest	
respect	rules	sadness	society	trap	white		

3 **Work in pairs and check your answers. Does Robert mention any words you chose in 1?**

 Now listen again and check.

4 **Work in pairs. Which of these statements do you agree or disagree with?**

1 A person should not show his or her feelings.
2 People are responsible for their own future.
3 Every group needs a leader.
4 Luck plays no part in our lives.
5 Criminals should be re-educated, not punished.
6 A spiritual life will compensate for deficiencies in everyday life.
7 Getting married is everyone's obligation.

5 **Match these comments from** *People Like Us* **with the statements in 4.**

a ☐ 'To a certain extent I agree. People who break the law need to realize that there are consequences for their actions, but at the same time, just punishing someone and not letting them know why it was wrong and why they should not do it again in the future, is not what should happen.' *Ben*

b ☐ 'Well, there is a Polish saying "People work out their destiny". But it's not true; not everybody has the same opportunities.' *Henryk*

c ☐ 'Yes, even though we have a sort of extended culture in the family, so there are other people who are responsible for your future. It's God's will first, and then you work on it.' *Deema*

d ☐ 'Sometimes hard work and luck go together. I think it's quite simple.' *James*

e ☐ 'I think this is normal, I think people should show their feelings.' *Ashura*

Speaking 6 **Look at this list of values and check (✓) the ones which are important to you.**

individualism	importance of the state	harmony	education
respect for age	personal space	equal opportunities	
face, reputation, and dignity	patriotism	freedom	honour	solidarity

7 **Work in pairs. Look at these symbols from banknotes, coins, and stamps from different countries. What cultural values do you think they represent?**

chatfile
4, 5, 6

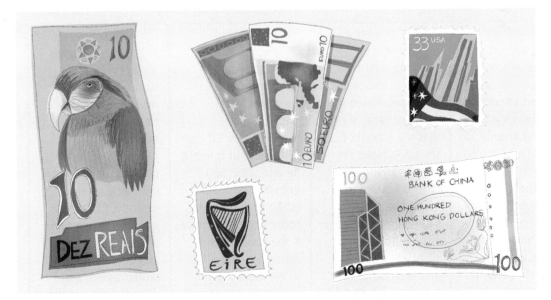

8 **Design your own banknote, coin, or stamp. Think of suitable cultural values to represent your country today.**

Vocabulary 1 **Work in pairs. Look at these two expressions about** *face.*

1 to lose face   2 to save face

Which of these words do you associate with each expression?

anger	dislike of saying no	disrespect	embarrassment
honor	kindness	reputation	status

Reading and Speaking 2 **Read some stories by Westerners about experiences in Asia. Which stories do the pictures show?**

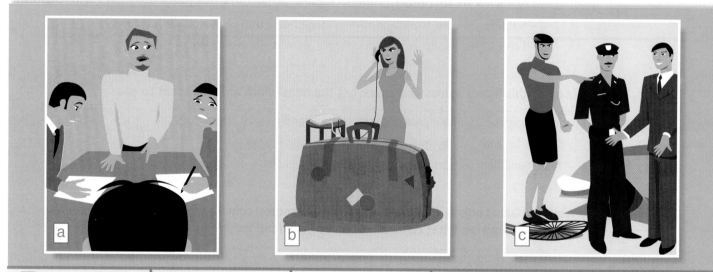

1 'I was walking along a street in Singapore when a man drove into a cyclist and knocked him off his bicycle. The cyclist wasn't hurt but he began to shout at the driver. A police officer arrived and listened carefully to the driver but ignored the cyclist, who was very angry and still shouting. It was clearly the driver's fault, but why didn't the police officer listen to the cyclist?'

2 'My teacher of Japanese was teaching us the names of countries and cities, when she said that New York was the capital of the USA. Now, I'm from Washington DC, so I raised my hand and politely said that she was wrong. She was silent for a moment, and then carried on teaching. What did I do wrong?'

3 'I invited my Singaporean friend to a dinner party at my apartment last Thursday. She replied, "Yes, I'd love to come, but it might be difficult." So I guessed she would either find a way to come or let me know if she couldn't. I didn't hear from her, so we were expecting her on Thursday, but she didn't come. Why didn't she call me?'

4 'One of my employees was always arriving late, so during a team meeting, when we'd finished the main business, I said, "Weimin, you've been getting to work late fairly often recently. Could you get to work on time, please?" Everyone looked very embarrassed, and since then, I get the impression that I did something wrong. Did I?'

5 'I'm going back to the UK next week, and a friend of mine asked if I could take something for his son who is studying there. It turned out to be a very heavy suitcase, so I decided to call him and say I couldn't take it. What else could I do?'

3 Work in pairs and discuss the situations in 2. Decide which of the aspects of *face* in 1 the situations show, and for whom.

Listening and Speaking **4** Listen to Barbara, an expert in cross-cultural communication, and check your answers.

5 Work in pairs and compare your answers. Can you remember in detail what Barbara said?

Now listen again and check.

6 Work in pairs and answer the questions.

1 What type of situation would cause someone to lose face in your country?
2 Do you ever lose your temper with people? If so, who?
3 How do you feel if someone loses their temper with you?
4 How can you avoid making others lose face?

7 Match Adriana's answers with the questions in 6.

8 Listen and check.

Adriana's answers

a ☐ 'It depends. If they are right, I apologize and try to correct the situation. If they are not right, I try to stay calm.'

b ☐ 'Here there is a lot of political corruption, but it's so common that people are not ashamed any more.'

c ☐ 'Trying to understand their situation, their point of view, their limitations, and trying to teach them.'

d ☐ 'Sometimes with people who don't know how to use simple services, and make things more complicated than they really are.'

Speaking **9** Work in pairs and answer the questions.

1 Can you think of situations in your culture when people might lose face?
2 What's the difference between face in the East and in the West?
3 Have you ever lost face? What happened?
4 Have you ever caused someone to lose face? What happened?

chatfile

3, 4, 5, 14

People Like You

1 **Work in pairs and answer the questions. Use some of these words to help you.**

brave	charming	cheerful	dishonest	friendly	generous	hard-working
honest	ignorant	intelligent	irritable	loud	outgoing	polite proud
racist	reserved	rude	shy	talkative	violent	welcoming

1 Look at the photos and decide where the people come from. What words would you use to describe people from these countries?

2 Have you met anyone from the countries in the photos, or been to those countries?

2 **Work in pairs and talk about your answers to these questions.**

How would you describe ... ?

1 ... people from your country
2 ... people from your town or region
3 ... people who are the same age as you

4 ... people who are older
5 ... your relatives
6 ... yourself

3 **Work in pairs and answer the questions.**

a How do you think people from other cultures and countries describe people from your country?

b How do you see yourself?

c How do you think others see you?

d What aspects of your culture are you proud of?

4 **Read this interview with Ben and decide where the questions in 3 go.**

Interviewer	(1) _____
Ben	I see myself as very outgoing and sociable and intelligent, and a good person.
Interviewer	What are the main characteristics of people from your country?
Ben	A lot of them are ignorant, and make statements when they have no idea what they are saying, and they should really take a look at how they lead their lives.
Interviewer	(2) _____
Ben	The same way that I see myself.
Interviewer	(3) _____
Ben	Oh, I don't think anyone likes us, because people think that America is represented by fat, ignorant people who are rude and think they are better than everyone else, which in some cases is true. I mean, in the city it's different because the city is full of worldly and really in-the-know type of people. But if you go where a lot of others are from, in the South and the Mid-West, they look at you, and they won't want to talk to you, you know, they're all racist and stuff like that. So, I guess I can see why other people from other countries don't really care about Americans.
Interviewer	(4) _____
Ben	That we are a very productive society and we know how to get things done. That doesn't mean that there are aspects of my country that I am not proud of though.

5 🔊 **Listen and check.**

6 **Work in pairs and answer the questions.**

1 Is Ben positive or negative about himself?
2 Is he positive or negative about Americans?
3 What distinction does he make about different Americans?
4 Do you agree with what Ben says about America?

7 **Work in pairs and answer the questions.**

1 Do you think it's fair or useful to have a stereotypical view of people from different cultures if you don't know them?
2 Do you think it's fair for other people to have a stereotypical view of you if they don't know you?
3 Do you think stereotypical views can ever be dangerous? What can happen?
4 How can we avoid negative stereotypical views?

chatfile
5, 6, 20

Find out what others in your class think.

Speaking and Reading 1 Work in groups. Look at these situations and say what might be unusual.

2 **Answer the questions. Now work in pairs and check your answers.**

1 You're going shopping and you want to buy the following: a pair of jeans, some aspirins, a cell phone, an English dictionary, some batteries. You also want to have something to eat, and you'd like to see a movie. Where is the best place for all of these in your town?

  a   A drugstore.

  b   A shopping mall.

  c   A department store.

  d   Separate stores, such as a bookstore, pharmacy, etc.

2 It's your father's 60th birthday. What do you say to him?

  a   Congratulations!

  b   Happy Birthday!

  c   I'm so sorry to hear your news.

  d   Your good health!

3 You have a good job in a government department, and your best friend asks if you can help her nephew get a job in the same department. What do you do?

  a   Explain you can't help.

  b   Smile but do nothing.

  c   Offer to send information about vacancies, but explain that others make decisions about suitable people.

  d   Do everything you can to get your friend's nephew a job.

4 You're working with a group of students on a project. Someone makes a suggestion which everyone agrees with, except you. What do you?

  a   Explain why you disagree and refuse to work with the others.

  b   Say nothing and work with the others.

  c   Express your reservations but work with the others.

  d   Work with another group.

5 You're in a bookstore and the sales clerk says you've stolen a book which is in your bag. He is going to call the police. You bought the book at another store and have the receipt. What do you do?

  a   Show the clerk the receipt and demand an apology.

  b   Keep quiet until the police arrive.

  c   Show the clerk the receipt.

  d   Shout at him and say you didn't steal the book.

6 You meet someone from a different culture who makes a number of generalizations about your cultural characteristics. You think he is stereotyping you. What do you do?

  a   Ignore him.

  b   Explain that a culture has many different aspects.

  c   Make generalizations about his cultural characteristics.

  d   Shout at him angrily.

3 **Choose one of the *People Like Us* who you think is interesting, or who you think you know well. Think about how he or she might answer the quiz.**

4 **Work in groups. Talk about how *People Like Us* might answer the quiz.**

Speaking   5 **Look at these topics from Units 19 – 26.**

going on vacation   shopping   special occasions   work customs
weddings   cultural identity and values   face   stereotyping

Choose two or three of the topics and talk about what might be interesting or different about them when you're with people from other cultures.

59

Speaking and Reading

1 **Work in pairs. Look at the photos and describe what's happening.**

2 **Read *Culture Clash*. Are the situations surprising or usual in your culture?**

CULTURE CLASH

1 'I had come half way round the world to negotiate a sale. I spent a whole day in a meeting with my clients, and at the end of it, I expected a decision. But instead, we just shook hands and said goodbye. That was three weeks ago, and I still haven't heard anything from them. Was it worth the trip?' *Ed*

2 'On a recent trip I met a new business partner and I gave him my business card. He apologized and said he had run out of his own cards. So he tore my card in half, wrote his name, address, and other details on the back of it, and gave it back to me. Am I right to think this was rude?' *Satoshi*

3 'I was in a meeting at an important client's office, who I had made an appointment to see. We didn't have much time, but during the meeting, we were interrupted all the time by various people, who walked in without knocking and demanded information and decisions from my host. We finished the meeting without finishing our business. Is this usual?' *Helen*

4 'We were finishing our negotiation over a major purchase and I asked for a moment to discuss with my co-workers. The salesman then offered me a sum of money to 'help me make my mind up'. I was quite shocked, because we don't usually accept bribes. I refused, but should I have accepted?' *Tom*

5 'I happened to be in the area of a major client, so I called by and asked to see her. The receptionist told me to call later and fix a date and a time, as the client never sees anyone without an appointment. Am I right to think this was rude?' *Maurizio*

Listening and Speaking 3 🔘 **Listen to Barbara, an expert in cross-cultural communication, explaining the culture clashes described in 2. How does she answer each person's question?**

4 **Work in pairs and check your answers.**

Speaking and Listening 5 **Answer these questions about meetings and negotiations. Put a check (✓) if you agree, a cross (✗) if you disagree, and (?) if you don't know.**

	You	Raj
1 Do people do business on the phone?		
2 Do people do business in a meeting?		
3 Do people do business in a restaurant?		
4 Do people make an appointment to see someone?		
5 Do people exchange business cards with people they meet for the first time?		
6 In a meeting do people expect others, who are not part of the meeting, to interrupt and discuss other business?		
7 Are the final decisions about deals and negotiations made by a team?		
8 Do people ever talk about personal matters when they're talking business?		
9 Is it helpful to offer a gift or money to ensure a successful negotiation?		

6 🔘 **Listen to Raj and put a check (✓) by the statements in 5 he agrees with.**

7 **Work in pairs and check your answers.
Can you remember in detail what Raj said?**

🔘 **Now listen again and check.**

Speaking 8 **Work in pairs and discuss your answers to the questions in 5. If you are from the same country as your partner, do you agree? If not, do you have any similar answers?**

chatfile
5, 6, 20

Vocabulary and Reading

1 **Look at the photos and say which holidays or festivals you can see.**

Buddha's birthday	Christmas	The Day of the Dead	Diwali	Easter
Eid	Father's Day	Halloween	Harvest	Holy Week	Independence Day
The King's/Queen's birthday	May Day	Mother's Day	New Year
Remembrance Day	St.Valentine's Day	Thanksgiving

2 **Read the *Calendar of Important Holidays and Festivals in Canada*.**
Which festivals in 1 do the Canadians celebrate?

Calendar of Important Holidays and Festivals in Canada

**Many public holidays in Canada
are on Friday or Monday,
so many people take advantage
of the long weekend and go away.**

1 January New Year's Day, a public holiday.

late March/April The date of Easter varies from year to year. It begins with Good Friday and finishes with Easter Monday. Special foods include hot cross buns and chocolate Easter eggs.

May The Monday before May 25 is Victoria Day, which celebrates Queen Victoria's birthday.

July 1 Canada Day. This is the anniversary of when the Dominion of Canada was created.

August August civic holiday. This marks the mid-point of the summer season.

September The first Monday in September is Labor Day. It marks the end of summer and the beginning of the school year.

October The Canadians hold Thanksgiving Day on the second Monday in October, and it's a celebration of the harvest.

31 October Halloween is not a public holiday, but an important event for children, who make lanterns from pumpkins, and dress up and go from house to house to collect candies.

11 November On Remembrance Day Canadians remember the war dead of the twentieth century.

25 December Christmas Day, when families get together and have Christmas dinner of turkey, ham, and Christmas pudding.

26 December Boxing Day, like Christmas Day, is a public holiday.

Listening and Speaking

3 Listen to *People Like Us* talking about holidays and festivals. Match each person to the holiday or festival they're talking about.

Adriana	Diwali
Valentina	Buddha's birthday
Henryk	Harvest
Chutima	mid-August holiday
Raj	Easter

4 Work in pairs and check your answers.

Reading and Listening

5 Read the interview with Ashura and decide where these questions go.

a What special food do you have?

b What's the most important religious or state festival in your country?

c Which festivals do you celebrate?

d What special customs and traditions do you have?

Interviewer	(1) _____
Ashura	We have many. I think they are both the same, we have Christian and Muslim festivals.
Interviewer	(2) _____
Ashura	We celebrate Christmas, New Year, Easter, Independence Day, Eid. And we have *Sabba Sabba* and we have *Nani Nani* – that's the celebration of harvest. And *Sabba Sabba* is the celebration of the formation of the Independence Party in Tanzania.
Interviewer	Which festivals do you celebrate with special food?
Ashura	We celebrate Eid.
Interviewer	(3) _____
Ashura	You must eat meat on this day. We prefer goat or chicken.
Interviewer	(4) _____
Ashura	I don't have any.

6 Listen and check.

Speaking

7 Work in pairs. Talk about important holidays and festivals in your country. Use the questions in 5 to help you.

chatfile
4, 5, 6, 18

Speaking and Reading 1 **Work in pairs and say what the jobs are in the photos. Do you expect the jobs to be done by men, women, or both?**

2 **Work in pairs. Read these statements and put a check (✓) if you agree, a cross (✗) if you disagree, and (?) if you don't know.**

	You	Deema
1 Few women are good enough to be top managers.		
2 Women should be paid the same as men for doing the same job.		
3 A husband should earn more than his wife.		
4 Boys are more highly regarded than girls.		
5 Women shouldn't work when they have children to look after.		
6 It's a woman's duty to marry and have children.		
7 It should be acceptable for a man to have a mistress.		
8 A wife should only have female friends.		
9 The husband should make all the important financial decisions.		
10 A wife should take her husband's salary and give him an allowance.		
11 It's a man's duty to protect the family.		
12 A husband and wife should share the housework.		

Listening and Speaking 3 **Listen to Deema talking about men and women. Put a check (✓) by the statements in 2 she agrees with. Which statements does she disagree with?**

4 **Work in pairs and check your answers.**

Reading and Speaking 5 **Read these situations. Are they likely to happen in your country?**

1 'My boss is always complimenting his female staff on their looks, their clothes and asking personal questions about their boyfriends or husbands. My female co-workers don't seem to mind, but I find his behavior rather rude. What can I do?'
Julia

2 'I travel a lot and often spend the evening on my own in a restaurant, which is fine. But there's always someone who thinks I look lonely and offers to buy me a drink. How can I explain politely but firmly that I'm happy with my own company?'
Ingrid

3 'I'm six months pregnant, and my partner and I don't mind if we have a boy or a girl. But we have several friends who, when we talk about the baby, make it clear that they wish me to have a boy. I realize there's a cultural difference but I don't know what to say.'
Aisha

5 'Some foreign business people have been over here negotiating a deal with my husband. When the meeting was over they invited him out for dinner, but they didn't invite me, even though I had met them. Should I feel insulted?'
Ok

4 'I have a boyfriend who is great fun to be with, but he continually holds doors open for me to go through first, or walks on the outside of the pavement, so I don't get splashed by the traffic, or offers to carry my bag and books back from university. I know he only wants to be polite, but I find his behavior sexist. Am I right?'
Isabella

6 **Work in pairs. What's the problem in each situation in 5?**
What advice would you give to each person?

Listening and Speaking 7 **Listen to Raj and Chutima answering these questions. What do they say?**

a Do you have many friends of the opposite sex?

b Does a man's behavior towards his wife change after they get married?

c Who looks after the family finances?

d Do most women have a job outside the household?

e Are there many women in managerial jobs?

f Are there certain jobs which only men or women do?

Now work in pairs and check your answers.

8 **Work in pairs and talk about men and women in your country.**
Answer the questions in 7. Are you like the *People Like Us*?

chatfile
5, 6, 19

1 **Work in pairs. Here are some words people use when they raise their glass and make a toast.**

| à votre santé | cheers | gan bei | prost | salud | salute | skol |

Match the words with the languages they come from. What do you say in your language?

English   French   German   Italian   Mandarin Chinese   Spanish   Swedish

2 **Read these expressions and number them in the order you might hear them during a meal.**

a Enjoy your meal! ☐   g It was delicious, but I've had enough. ☐
b Can I pass you anything? ☐   h Help yourself. ☐
c Sit anywhere you like. ☐   i This is delicious. ☐
d Come and sit down. ☐   j Where would you like me to sit? ☐
e Please start. ☐   k Could you pass the salt, please? ☐
f Would you like some more? ☐   l Just a little for me, please. ☐

3 **Look at the photo. What do you think the man who is standing up is doing? Turn to page 81 to find out.**

4 **Describe the ritual of making a toast in your culture.**

Reading and Listening

5 Look at the pictures of different table manners around the world. Which are acceptable in your culture?

6 Read the questionnaire about table manners and think about your answers.

1 You're invited to dinner with friends or business acquaintances. Is it usual to entertain people at home or in a restaurant?

2 What time do they invite you for? What time do you arrive?

3 What happens before you eat?

4 Where do people sit at the table?

5 Who is served first?

6 Do you start eating as soon as you're served?

7 Where do you put your hands when you're not eating?

8 Is it acceptable to refuse something you don't want to eat?

9 Do you eat everything on your plate?

10 If you don't want any more food, how do you show this?

11 Is it usual to make noises while you're eating?

12 How do you know when to leave?

7 Listen to *People Like Us* talking about table manners. Decide which questions in the questionnaire they're answering.

Deema ☐ ☐ ☐   Raj ☐ ☐ ☐
Ben ☐   Ashura ☐ ☐ ☐
Adriana ☐   Chutima ☐

Now work in pairs and check your answers.

chatfile
5, 6, 19

Speaking

8 Work in pairs and talk about your answers to the questionnaire in 6. Are you like the *People Like Us*?

32 School

Speaking and Vocabulary 1 **Look at the photos. Where do you think these students come from?**

2 **Work in pairs. Check (✓) the features and facilities a typical school in your country has.**

☐ classrooms   ☐ auditorium   ☐ playground

☐ sports field   ☐ swimming pool   ☐ gymnasium

☐ library   ☐ cafeteria   ☐ vending machine for snacks

☐ basketball court   ☐ tennis court   ☐ dormitories

3 **Number the features and facilities that you checked in 2, from 1 (most important) to the least important.**
Now work in pairs and compare your answers.

Reading and Listening 4 **Read the interview with Adriana about the education system and schools in Brazil. Write the questions the interviewer asked.**

Interviewer (1) _____

Adriana It depends on the family, but usually around 18 months or two years old. But compulsory school begins at seven.

Interviewer (2) _____

Adriana Well, according to the law, they spend eight years at school, so they can leave when they're fifteen. But in most cases, this doesn't happen.

Interviewer (3) _____

Adriana They have a break once a day because most schools only offer half-time study. The children finish class and go home at lunch time, or they have lunch at home and then go to school.

Interviewer (4) _____

Adriana Yes, sometimes, if they are full-time, they eat a lunch prepared at the school cafeteria.

Interviewer (5) _____

Adriana Generally 40, but this number varies according to the school.

Interviewer (6) _____

Adriana Yes, English is compulsory from eleven years old.

Interviewer (7) _____

Adriana When they finish high school, there is an important university entrance exam.

Interviewer (8) _____

Adriana Most people study at the university where they are offered a place, not their local one.

5 **Listen and check.**

Listening and Speaking 6 **Work in groups of three. You're going to hear Henryk and Ashura. Student A: Turn to page 78. Student B: Turn to page 79. Student C: Turn to page 80.**

7 **Work in your groups and complete the chart.**

	Henryk	Ashura
Compulsory schooling		
Break times and school lunch		
Class size		
Main exams and university		

chatfile
5, 6

8 **Work in pairs and talk about the education system and schools in your country. Use the questions you wrote in 4 to help you.**

33 Homeland

Speaking and Listening **1 Work in pairs and answer the questions.**

1 Where is your *home*? Is it where you live, where you were born, or where your parents live/lived?
2 Would you like to live in another country? If so, where and why? If not, why not?

2 Listen to Jamie, who's Scottish, and check (✓) the true statements.

1 Jamie was born in Glasgow. ☐
2 He was born in Inverness. ☐
3 His mother's family is from Italy. ☐
4 He'd like to live in Italy. ☐
5 He doesn't like the weather in Scotland. ☐
6 He likes visiting his family in Rome. ☐

3 Work in pairs and check your answers. Can you remember in detail what Jamie said?

Now listen again and check.

Reading and Listening

4 **Read these exchanges from an interview with Valentina and number them in the correct order. The first one has been done for you.**

a ☐ **Interviewer** In your country, would you say there are a lot of people from different ethnic backgrounds?

b ☐1 **Interviewer** When someone asks where you are from, do you say your town or your village or your region or your country?

c ☐ **Interviewer** What sort of ethnic background do people come from?

d ☐ **Valentina** I say Italy and then I say Sicily and then I say Sciacca and then I start explaining where Sciacca is. Once someone asked me and I said Sicily, and then they asked me if Sicily was in Europe! So now I always say Italy.

e ☐ **Valentina** Not in Sicily, but in the regions that make up Italy, especially in the north.

f ☐ **Valentina** In the south they are more Mediterranean, more like Spanish people. Northerners are more like Germans or Austrians.

5 🔘 **Listen and check.**

6 **Match these questions with Henryk and Ashura's answers.**

1 When someone asks where you're from, do you say your village or town, your region, or your country? ☐ ☐

2 Are there people from different ethnic backgrounds in your country? ☐ ☐

a 'Yes, there are, many tribes. We have 125 regions, and each region can have more than three tribes.' *Ashura*

b 'It depends where I am. If I were in my country, I would tell them my region. And when I am in someone else's country, I would tell them which country I come from.' *Ashura*

c 'People say their hometown first and if it's a village or a small town then they sometimes say the region to indicate where it is situated.' *Henryk*

d 'Yes, you can see it more and more. But people from ethnic minorities are largely adapted to and assimilated in the social, economic, and political reality in Poland. They don't have representatives in the government, but do in parliament.' *Henryk*

7 🔘 **Listen and check.**

Speaking **8** **Work in pairs and answer the questions about homeland in 4. Are you like the *People Like Us*?**

chatfile
5, 6, 19

1 **Look at the photos. Do you know what they show?**

2 **Work in pairs. Student A: Turn to page 78. Student B: Turn to page 79.**

3 **Check (✓) the statements you agree with.**

1 It's very important to know how old someone is. ☐
2 I never call older people by their first name. ☐
3 When people retire, they should stop work and enjoy themselves. ☐
4 Older people should step aside and let younger people take over. ☐
5 I share my opinions freely with older people. ☐
6 Older people speak very directly to younger people. ☐

4 **Work in pairs and talk about your answers. Do you both agree?**

Reading and Listening 5 **Think about your answers to these questions.**

1 At what age do working people retire in your country?
2 Do retired people continue to play a role in society or in the family?
3 How are old people considered by younger people?
4 Who looks after elderly people who are seriously ill?
5 Are there any rituals or customs to show respect for your ancestors?

6 **Match these comments by** *People Like Us* **with the questions in 5.**

a ☐ 'Men retire when they are 65, and women when they are 60.' *Henryk*

b ☐ 'We give food to the monk and the monk prays. After that, we write down the name of the ancestor on a piece of paper and the monk reads aloud. When the monk is praying we pour the water. It means that we give all things to them. After, we take the water and put it under a big tree to go into the ground.' *Chutima*

c ☐ 'They respect them.' *Chutima*

d ☐ 'Yes. I am a Muslim, but I don't follow what Muslims do. In my tribe we respect snakes. When I was at my grandmother's house we saw a snake and she said, "Wait, this snake is our ancestor come to greet us." So she mixed maize flour and water and she put it before the snake and the snake started eating it. I was so scared; it was a very big python. But I don't believe in that. You cannot tell me a snake is my relative.' *Ashura*

e ☐ 'The children. If you put them in a nursing home – you don't respect a family who have done that, because it is rude towards those elderly people. It is very rare.' *Deema*

f ☐ 'We always choose the one in the family who gets less pay than the others to stay at home and look after them.' *Chutima*

g ☐ '*Ching Ming*, usually they like to go to their father's tomb and clean it and take some cakes, and maybe some paper to burn. Actually this is money for the dead people.' *James*

h ☐ 'Yes, they do. Normally when a person retires we believe that he or she is a person with wisdom that can advise young people in the street, maybe.' *Ashura*

i ☐ 'The children have a legal responsibility for the parents, but more and more often well-off people leave elderly and ill people to retirement homes.' *Henryk*

j ☐ 'The son or the children.' *Hiromi*

7 🔘 **Listen and check.**

Speaking 8 **Work in pairs and answer the questions about elderly people and ancestors in 5. Are you like the** *People Like Us***?**

chatfile
5, 6, 19

35 Time

1 Work in pairs and answer the questions.

1 What time did your lesson start?
2 What time does the lesson finish?
3 What time will you leave?
4 What time is it now?
5 What time did you get to school/college today?
6 What time will you get home?

2 Read the questionnaire and think about your answers.

DO YOU LIVE IN A CLOCK-TIME WORLD OR A RIGHT-TIME WORLD?

Some people organize their lives around the clock. When it's 11:00 p.m., they go to bed. Some people do things when it's the right time for them – they go to bed when they're tired. Answer the questions and find out if you live in a clock-time world or a right-time world.

1 When do you have lunch?
 a When I'm hungry.
 b At a specific time of day eg 12:30 p.m.

2 When does your class start?
 a When everyone is here.
 b At a specific time, eg 10:00 a.m.

3 When you have a business appointment for 9:00 a.m., when do you arrive?
 a After 9:00 a.m.
 b 9:00 a.m. exactly.
 c Before 9:00 a.m.

4 You're invited to a dinner party for 8:00 p.m. When do you arrive?
 a 9:00 a.m.
 b 8:10 – 8:15 p.m.
 c 7:45 p.m.

5 You're late for a class or an appointment. How late do you have to be to apologize?
 a 10 minutes. b 5 minutes.
 c 2 minutes.

6 When were you born?
 a I know the date.
 b I know the date and the exact time.

7 You're walking in the country. You meet someone who asks you how far a village is. How do you answer?
 a not far. b one hour. c five miles.

8 When does night stop and morning begin?
 a When the sun rises.
 b When I get up.
 c At 7:00 a.m.

9 When does summer begin?
 a When it gets hot.
 b In June.
 c In December.

10 You ask an engineer to fix your telephone. He says he'll do it as soon as possible. When do you expect this to be?
 a no idea.
 b in a week or more.
 c in a day or two.

11 When do people finish work in your culture?
 a When the work is done.
 b Around a specific time, eg 5:00 – 5:30 p.m.
 c At an exact time, eg 5:00 p.m.

12 You're waiting to see someone very important. How long do you expect to wait?
 a A very long time.
 b A short time.
 c No time at all.

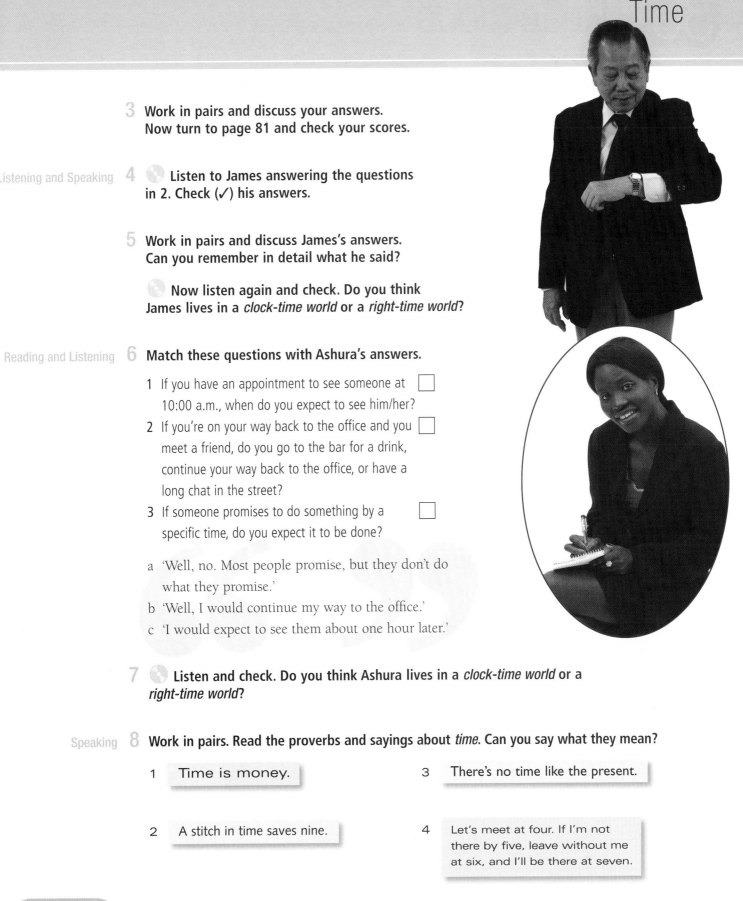

3 Work in pairs and discuss your answers.
Now turn to page 81 and check your scores.

Listening and Speaking

4 Listen to James answering the questions in 2. Check (✓) his answers.

5 Work in pairs and discuss James's answers. Can you remember in detail what he said?

Now listen again and check. Do you think James lives in a *clock-time world* or a *right-time world*?

Reading and Listening

6 Match these questions with Ashura's answers.

1 If you have an appointment to see someone at 10:00 a.m., when do you expect to see him/her? ☐

2 If you're on your way back to the office and you meet a friend, do you go to the bar for a drink, continue your way back to the office, or have a long chat in the street? ☐

3 If someone promises to do something by a specific time, do you expect it to be done? ☐

a 'Well, no. Most people promise, but they don't do what they promise.'
b 'Well, I would continue my way to the office.'
c 'I would expect to see them about one hour later.'

7 Listen and check. Do you think Ashura lives in a *clock-time world* or a *right-time world*?

Speaking

8 Work in pairs. Read the proverbs and sayings about *time*. Can you say what they mean?

1 Time is money.

2 A stitch in time saves nine.

3 There's no time like the present.

4 Let's meet at four. If I'm not there by five, leave without me at six, and I'll be there at seven.

chatfile
5, 6, 17

Now talk about the proverbs in 8. What cultural values do they suggest? Have you got any proverbs about time in your language? Can you translate them into English?

Speaking and Reading   1   **Work in groups. Look at these situations and say what might be unusual.**

2 **Answer the questions. Now work in pairs and check your answers.**

1 A friend has invited you to celebrate an important religious festival with her. You're not of the same religion. It involves some religious customs and a family meal. What should you do?
a   Join in and ask her for advice on what you should do.
b   Refuse politely and stay at home.
c   Go to the meal but don't join in the religious customs.
d   Pretend you're busy.

2 When someone you don't know asks where you're from, where do you say you're from?
a   The village or town where you live.
b   The nearest big city.
c   The region where you live.
d   Your country.

3 You're having the first meeting with a new business partner. What do you talk about?
a   Your business plans.
b   Personal matters, such as your family and your home.
c   Personal matters, and your business plans.
d   Nothing important.

4 Your friend tells you she is pregnant. What do you think?
a   I hope she has a boy.
b   I hope her child is healthy.
c   I hope she has a girl.
d   If she has a girl, maybe she'll have a boy next time.

5 You're having dinner with friends. You've finished eating what they've prepared for you. What happens next?
a   You get up and say goodbye.
b   You carry on talking and drinking.
c   You accept a cup of coffee or tea and then leave.
d   You wait until they ask you to leave.

6 Your father is sixty and about to retire. What do you think?
a   My brothers and sisters will make sure he enjoys his retirement.
b   He'll carry on as head of the family but won't have to do anything.
c   We'll take over all his responsibilities.
d   The eldest son is now in charge.

3 **Choose one of the *People Like Us* who you think is interesting, or who you think you know well. Think about how he or she might answer the quiz.**

4 **Work in groups. Talk about how *People Like Us* might answer the quiz.**

Speaking   5 **Look at these topics from Units 28 – 35.**

meetings and negotiations   holidays and festivals   men and women
table manners   school   homeland   ancestors   time

Choose two or three of the topics and talk about what might be interesting or different about them when you're with people from other cultures.

Communication Activities

Student A

7.6 Ask and answer the questions in 1. Follow the instructions on how to behave below.

> **Aspects of behavior**
> Keep smiling and touching Student B, and sit close. Try to keep the conversation going. Ask lots of questions and repeat each answer in a different way to make sure you have understood.

12.6 Read the text about leisure activities in the USA.

Baseball, basketball, American football, and ice-hockey are the most popular spectator and participation sports, but Americans enjoy an enormous range of activities, including soccer, cycling, racket-ball (a hybrid of squash and handball), tennis, swimming, fishing, golf, bowling, martial arts, walking, jogging, and aerobic exercise. Schools, cities, and other organizations sponsor team sports for young people, and professional sports are an important part of the culture. In general, most Americans spend a large amount of their leisure time socializing or watching television. Other leisure activities include going to the movies or concerts, picnicking, and traveling. Many Americans volunteer for a wide range of causes, from raising funds to helping those who are less fortunate, tutoring students or leading Scout troops and youth sports. Even city dwellers enjoy spending time in the 'great outdoors', camping, hiking, or hunting.

Now turn back to page 29.

23.5 Listen and find out:

– what Chutima says about special customs and traditions
– what Chutima says happens after the ceremony
– what Deema says happens before the ceremony
– what Deema says about typical gifts

32.6 Listen and find out:

– what Henryk says about compulsory schooling
– what Henryk says about main exams and university
– what Ashura says about class size

34.2 Write questions about the missing information. Now work in pairs. Ask and answer questions about *The Day of the Dead*, and complete the paragraphs.

The Day of the Dead

(1)_____ is on 2 November and is known in Mexico as *The Day of the Dead*. It's a festival which dates back to (3)_____. According to the Mexicans, they believe that the souls of the dead come back to the earth on this day to visit (5)_____. So people go to the cemeteries to take (7)_____. They also take candles, and special foods such as candy in the shape of skulls, hearses, and coffins. There are also (9)_____ alongside the rituals in the cemeteries. However, it's not a sad occasion. It's more of a celebration of the lives of family and friends who have died. The idea is that death is not an ending, but simply another stage of life.

Communication Activities

Student B

7.6 Ask and answer the questions in 1. Follow the instructions on how to behave below.

> **Aspects of behavior**
> Answer Student A's questions, but only give the essential information. Don't look at Student A. You don't like people touching you, but you're too polite to say anything.

12.6 Read the text about leisure activities in Russia.

While wealthier urban Russians often have a cottage in the country, called a *dacha*, to which they go for weekends and vacations, many Russians have to devote much of their leisure time to getting food, taking on extra jobs, and looking after their households. Soccer is the favorite sport but others, particularly winter sports such as ice-skating, ice-hockey, and cross-country skiing, are also popular. Playing chess is a favorite pastime.

Watching television is another common leisure activity, and even small towns have theaters and movie theaters. Rural people can watch movies at a *dvorets kultury* (a 'palace of culture'), which serves as a community recreation centre. Market forces have also resulted in the establishment of a lively nightclub scene in cities such as Moscow and St.Petersburg.

Now turn back to page 29.

23.5 Listen and find out:

– what Chutima says about typical gifts
– what Chutima says happens before the ceremony
– what Deema says happens during the ceremony

32.6 Listen and find out:

– what Henryk says about break times and school lunch
– what Ashura says about compulsory schooling
– what Ashura says about main exams and university

34.2 Write questions about the missing information. Now work in pairs. Ask and answer questions about *The Day of the Dead*, and complete the paragraphs.

The Day of the Dead

All Souls' Day is on (2)_____ and is known in Mexico as *The Day of the Dead*. It's a festival which dates back to before Christian times. According to the Mexicans, they believe that the (4)_____ come back to the earth on this day to visit friends and family. So people go to (6)_____ to take flowers to the graves. They also take (8)_____ such as candy in the shape of skulls, hearses, and coffins. There are also parades, markets, and concerts alongside the rituals in the cemeteries. However, it's not a sad occasion. It's more of a celebration of (10)_____. The idea is that death is not an ending, but simply another stage of life.

Student C

12.6 **Read the text about leisure activities in Australia.**

Australians have a passion for sport, and outdoor activities are an important part of Australian life. Australian Rules football is the country's main spectator sport, followed by rugby and cricket (Australia's national teams are among the best in the world). Association soccer and horse-racing are also popular. Australians enjoy a wide range of other sports, including basketball, netball (similar to basketball, but played almost exclusively by women), cycling, bush-walking, golf, tennis, and lawn bowls. With the majority of Australians living on or near the coast, there is great enthusiasm for sailing, surfing, swimming, and fishing. Australians watch a great deal of television, and movies are also popular.

Now turn back to page 29.

23.5 **Listen and find out:**

– what Chutima says happens during the ceremony
– what Deema says about special customs and traditions
– what Deema says happens after the ceremony

32.6 **Listen and find out:**

– what Henryk says about class size
– what Ashura says about break times and school lunch

Communication Activities

All students

Read the text and answer the questions.

1 Who is the man standing up?
2 What's his role?
3 Who or what does he make toasts to?
4 What should the men do?
5 What should the women do?
6 How long does this ritual go on?
7 What's the most interesting or surprising piece of information?

> Traditionally, before a meal, the Tamada (a toastmaster) is chosen from among the people present. The Tamada is always a man, and he is usually either the host or a close friend of the host, and in a position to greet and welcome the other guests. He proposes toasts to anything from national values to each individual at the table, the importance of the occasion or even the beauty of the women and the intelligence of the men round the table ... and drinks the entire glass after each toast. Men are expected to follow the Tamada in emptying their glasses, but women only have to make a show of drinking. It is improper to drink alcohol without first proposing a toast. This ritual of toasts continues through the whole meal, and each time the guests raise their glasses.

35.3 **Mostly a's**
You live in a right-time world.

Mostly b's and c's
You live in a clock-time world.

Somewhere between the two
You live in the real world!

Unit Notes

 Greetings

In this unit we look at the different ways people greet each other in different cultures and talk about how formal or informal we need to be with family, friends, and people we've just met.

Activity 3

We say *Good morning* until midday, *good afternoon* until about 6:00 p.m. and *good evening* until midnight. We only use *good night* to say *goodbye*.

Good day is the most common expression in Australian English for *hello*. You don't hear it very often in American English, except as a formal *goodbye*.

Remember that you say *How do you do?* when you meet someone for the first time, and the correct response is *How do you do?* You can also say *Pleased to meet you.*

How are you? is a friendly greeting and not a genuine inquiry about your health. In other parts of the world, such as South-East Asia, you might hear *Where are you going?* or *Have you eaten?*

Activity 5

Remember that people from some cultures, such as North America, often invite someone they've just met to use their given name, *Please call me Ginny.*

Activity 7

Raj lives in Gujarat, a state in western India, which has absorbed customs from people from the many different cultures from the East and from the West who have lived there.

Look at activity 1, photo 5 to see a *namaste*.

Raj uses the word *professor* to mean all teachers, although in US English, this means a teacher at a university.

 Name and Address

In this unit, we look at different forms of titles and names, ways of describing where people live, and how parents choose their children's names.

Activity 1

There are sometimes important differences in how people describe where they live, which may make it difficult to understand the details of the address. For example, in the USA, we put the house or apartment number before the street name; in Brazil it goes after the street name. In Poland, the city or town and the zip code comes on the line below the person's name. In some countries writing the name and address correctly is a legal requirement if you expect your mail to be delivered successfully.

Activity 2

zip code (US) = *post code* (UK)

Activity 4

In formal situations in some cultures, it's important to use the person's rank or title, or job title when you address them. In the USA, we might say, for example, *Doctor* or *Professor Smith*, but we don't say *Teacher* or *Engineer Smith*.

We never use *Mr., Mrs., Miss* or *Ms.* without saying their family name.

Remember that you pronounce *Mr.* as 'mister' and *Mrs.* as 'mizzuz' or 'missiz'. You pronounce *Ms.* as 'mizz', and many women choose this title because it doesn't show if the person is married or not.

Activity 5

In US English we use the term *first name* instead of *given name*, because it always comes before the *family name* or *last name*. In many cultures, the given name (the name given by the parents or family) does not come in first position. For example, a Chinese person might be called *Mao Dun* : his family name is *Mao*, and his given name is *Dun*.

A *nickname* is a short version of someone's name (for example, *Bill* for *William, Liz* for *Elizabeth*), or a name people have invented for someone. We always use it affectionately and with the person's agreement.

Activity 7

fortune-teller = someone who can tell what is going to happen in the future

Chutima mentions *vowels* and *consonants*. In English there are five vowels: *a, e, i, o* and *u*. All the other letters in the alphabet are consonants.

3 Home Comforts

This unit looks at living conditions and typical homes in different cultures.

Activity 1

A *house* is a building where a single group of people, such as a family, live. It usually has more than one floor. An *apartment* (UK *flat*) is a set of rooms within a building and usually on one floor.

Activity 2

renovated = something made as good as new

suburbs = the area around a city, often where people live

subway (US) = the underground railroad in a city. The *metro* is also the underground railroad, but is used for cities such as Paris or Moscow. In UK English, the London subway/metro system is called *the underground* or *the tube*.

Activity 4

James refers to *Feng Shui*, which is the Chinese study of the relationship between our environment, especially where we live and work, and the spiritual forces which influence it.

Raj refers to *retirement*, which is when older people stop working. The *ancestral home* is where your ancestors lived.

Henryk says *rent a flat*. This means to pay the owner money to live in an apartment, but not to buy it. A *pensioner* is a British English word for someone who is retired and who receives money from the state or lives on their savings.

Activity 7

essential = something which, in your opinion, you need

luxury = something which is good to have, but which you may not need

 ## 4 Buying Food

In this unit we look at different customs in shopping for food, and in particular, who does the shopping, what people typically buy, and where they go to buy it.

Activity 1

In the USA, we don't use the metric system, but US measures for weights and liquids.

Activity 3

A *market* is usually in a special building (a covered market) or in the street, and sells fresh meat, fish, dairy produce, fruit, and vegetables. A *supermarket* is a large store which sells food, either frozen or in cans, and drink, and fresh food.

trash = paper and other dry waste which you throw away. It can also mean the place where you put it. *Garbage* refers to kitchen waste.

Activity 6

In Spain and some other countries, men go shopping for bread early in the morning while their wives are getting the family and breakfast ready.

stall = a temporary table, sometimes with a roof, where you buy produce at a market

bargain = negotiate the price of something. In some cultures, such as in the Arab world, it's common to bargain with shopkeepers. In others, such as in the USA and most of Europe, it's not acceptable, except for certain goods.

A *stall-holder* is the person who serves at the stall. At the end of the market, the stallholder takes down the stall.

stand in line = wait your turn for someone to serve you or, for example, to get on a bus

siesta is a Spanish word to describe the period during the afternoon, from about 1:00 p.m. to 5:00 p.m., when shops and offices are closed, usually because of the heat, and people are resting. We often use the word in English.

hypermarket = a huge supermarket on a single floor, which is situated outside the town. It will always sell food. A department store is usually on several floors and situated downtown, but may not always sell food.

5 Family Life

In this unit we look at the structure of the family in different cultures, and especially at the number of members of a family who live together, relationships within the family, family responsibilities, and marriage customs.

Activity 1

single-parent family = a family in which the children only live with one parent

unmarried partners are a couple who live together. They may even have children, but are not married. This is quite common in the USA and much of Europe.

divorced = when a marriage is over and the two partners legally separate

step-parents: A *step-mother* is not your real mother, but is married to your real father; a *step-father* is not your real father, but is married to your real mother.

half-brothers and sisters = the sons or daughters of your mother or father by a different partner

Activity 2

Algeria is the fifth largest country in the world, and the largest in Africa. Eighty-five per cent of it is covered by the Sahara desert, so most of the population, which is largely Muslim, lives on the Mediterranean coast.

generation = a group of people who were born at approximately the same time and are considered as having similar attitudes and interests. You often talk about *the older generation*, *the younger generation* and *the generation gap*.

family income = the money a family needs to live

Activity 4

As you will remember, Deema who is 35, is from Jordan. She's a Muslim.

Mum (UK) = an affectionate term for *mother*. (US *Mom*)

she is not physically up to it = she's not able to do it because she's physically weak

pass away = die

Unit Notes

 Dating

This unit is about the customs of meeting friends of the opposite sex in different cultures and of choosing one's marriage partner.

Activity 1

Some of the expressions, such as *cute* and *ex* are informal, and in more formal circumstances it may be more appropriate to use the definitions.

Activity 4

Many US TV programs are about young people meeting and making friends, so people are more exposed to US dating customs than those of other cultures. You may like to think of a popular US TV program such as *Friends*, and discuss what changes you might make so that it shows dating customs in your culture.

teenager = a boy or a girl who is between the ages of thir*teen* and nine*teen*. We've used this word since about 1935–40, and it also suggests the state of emotional and intellectual development between being a child and an adult.

Activity 6

Henryk is 75, which he thinks is old, and which explains why he thinks he has outgrown dating.

kindergarten = the first school children go to, perhaps from the age of five or six

chaperone = a parent or a teacher who oversees a school dance or a party

deadline = the latest time you have to be home or to finish something

 Personal Space

This unit looks at some of the conventions we observe in physical relationships with other people, such as how close we stand to people, making conversation with strangers, and other aspects of body language.

Activity 1

Some people belong to cultures where it's acceptable to stand or sit close to people, or to touch them. Latin America, southern Europe and the Arab World are close-contact cultures. Other people, such as North Americans, North Europeans and East and South-East Asians prefer to keep their distance. Sometimes, even if you're speaking fluent English, it's difficult to communicate with people from a different culture, and even if you are unable or unwilling to adjust your cultural characteristics, it's important to be aware of what's happening.

People in some cultures like to use distance between themselves and others as a way of marking their personal space. Some like to look people in the eye, as a mark of honesty. People from other cultures may be very happy to start conversations with complete strangers, or look away from people as a mark of respect. Sometimes these differences in behavior are not national, regional or local characteristics, but part of one's personal identity.

co-worker = someone you work with, but don't know well

waiting room = a room where you wait to see the doctor or dentist, or wait for your train

crowded = full of people

library = a place where you borrow books. A *bookshop* is a store where you buy books.

Activity 6

This role-play is designed to help you imagine what it's like when you meet someone from another culture with different behavior and customs, and where non-verbal aspects get in the way of effective communication.

 Gestures and Customs

This unit continues to explore the area of non-communication which we looked at in Unit 7. It examines gestures of the body, and if they are appropriate in all situations.

Activity 1

Some of these gestures, such as the male kiss, are common in Latin countries and Russia. In other cultures, such as China, they are unacceptable, and may cause offense. Some gestures may simply be unusual, but are not taboo. In the USA, people don't bow when they meet each other; in Japan, a bow is very common.

Activity 3

Deema uses the expression *body people*. She means that in her culture, people use their bodies to express themselves.

Henryk says *Yes, and only!* He means that men only kiss each other on the cheeks, and not on the lips.

Activity 6

the sign of the cross = the gesture Catholics make when they enter and leave a church. It's a way of paying respect to God.

incense = something you burn for its pleasant smell. People often use it in religious ceremonies.

In Arab countries, a traditional gesture of greeting or saying goodbye would be to shake hands and then to touch your heart with the palm of your right hand.

Activity 7

Remember that sometimes an innocent gesture in one culture may be rude in another. For example, an American might relax at work with his feet on his desk, or suggest everything is OK by making a ring with his thumb and forefinger. In other cultures, these are rude gestures.

It isn't possible to learn the meaning of all gestures in different cultures, but the most important thing is to be aware that the meaning might be different.

Activity 8

tell lies = not to tell the truth

be forgiven = God will forget the lies you have told

hitch a lift = to stand by the roadside and ask drivers to take you free of charge to where you want to go. US = *hitchhike*

obscene = very rude

victorious soldiers = soldiers who have won a battle or a war. Their *prisoners* are the enemy who they have captured.

dirt = earth or mud, or anything which isn't clean

 The Language of Clothes

This unit explores the kind of clothes people wear in different cultures and in different situations. It looks at the cultures where people still wear national dress, and on which occasions.

Activity 1

There are several differences between US and UK English words for clothes, which may cause some confusion. *Pants* (US) are *trousers* (UK); *shorts* (US) are *pants* (UK). *Shorts* in American and British English also means *short trousers*. *Vest* (US) is a jacket without sleeves, and in British English it's something you wear under your shirt (an *undershirt* in American English).

Activity 2

People's choice of clothes for different circumstances shows not only the impression they want to give other people but also their respect for the situation. What you wear to relax in at home is usually very different to what you wear for a job interview or a wedding. Your clothes are an important part of your non-verbal communication with others.

Activity 3

In many countries, people regularly wear their regional or national costume. For example, in Japan, it's common to see women going to a social event wearing kimonos. However, most cultures abandon their traditional dress in favor of more practical Western-style clothes. In some cultures, it's hard to decide what traditional dress might be.

Activity 4

India is an example of a country where people wear a mixture of Western-style clothes and traditional dress. Although Western clothes may be more practical in some ways, traditional dress is probably better suited to the Indian climate.

Activity 5

casual = relaxed or informal

Women wear *bangles* (US *bracelets*) on the wrists, *necklaces* around their necks, *rings* on their fingers and *earrings* in the ears. Men may sometimes wear rings and in some cultures, earrings. Do men wear rings and earrings in your culture?

In India, parts of Africa and Asia, the color of death is white. In other cultures, such as Europe and North and South America, the color is black.

11 Replying

In this unit we look at different comments, replies, and responses to different situations. The expressions we look at are often very short pieces of language, but they are all very much part of everyday interaction between people. In fact, if you don't use some of these expressions when an appropriate occasion arises, the person you're speaking to might feel something is missing in your conversation.

Activity 1

In the UK it might seem that people say *sorry* very often, and sometimes when it's not necessary to apologize. In Japanese *sumimasen* means both *thank you* and *sorry*.

You say *excuse me* to attract someone's attention, to interrupt someone, or to apologize for something minor, such as when you bump into someone in a crowded place. You also say it when you didn't hear something.

You use *thank you* very often in English, and although the expression exists in all languages, the frequency with which you say it is also important.

Hello is a neutral (neither formal nor informal) greeting.

Hey! is an informal, even rude, way of attracting someone's attention.

Pardon me is similar to *excuse me*.

You're welcome is what you say in reply to *thank you*.

Come here! is a strong order unless the gesture and other body language suggests an invitation.

Ouch! is what you say when something hurts you.

Please. is used very often in English, and in circumstances where you may not use it in your own language.

Unit Notes

Activity 2

You may think the customer and the shop assistant in Situation 3 are very polite to each other, but this is very common in shops in Britain and the USA, and if you don't use the expressions in a similar way, people may think you're rude.

Activity 4

Deema says *give the person a look*. This means to look at the person in an angry way, but without saying anything.

Activity 5

All these expressions are common in different cultures. For example, in certain cultures it's acceptable to praise someone by telling them they've put on weight, but in other cultures, this would be rude. *You look awful!* may be meant as a sympathetic comment to someone who looks ill, but it may not be understood in this way. *How much did it cost?* may appear to be an embarrassing question, but some people like to be open about the value of their possessions. As in many circumstances, the response will vary from individual to individual, as well as from culture to culture.

Activity 7 and Activity 8

These two activities consider the meaning of silence. It's usually rare for people to remain silent when they're with other people unless they know them extremely well. Long silences are either embarrassing or deeply meaningful, and most people try to avoid them. But there are occasions in many cultures where silence is acceptable or unavoidable. Sometimes it may be a religious occasion, sometimes it may be in an educational context, such in a class or in an exam, or sometimes in a business situation.

Activity 9

Some people apologize often for all sorts of minor inconveniences they may have caused other people. Other people choose to say nothing when an apology might be expected. If someone expects an apology which doesn't come, they may think the other person is being rude.

12 Time Off

This unit looks at the different ways people spend their leisure time. As we have already seen, our cultural identity consists of many features: the country or region where we live, our age, our social background, our economic status, our gender, and in this unit, our climate plays an important role in what we do to entertain ourselves.

Activity 1

You may like to think about which leisure activities in the list are outdoor ones, and what climate you need. Which do people do in your country?

Activity 3

Valentina talks about *football* (UK), which means *soccer* (US) and is played with a round ball. *Football* (US) is played with an oval ball.

Valentina mentions that in her culture everyone goes for a walk in the evening. This is the Italian custom of the promenade. People usually dress up in the early evening and go for a walk, perhaps around the town square, to meet friends and talk. This custom is common in many north Mediterranean countries.

In the West, Friday is the last day of the working week for most people, and Saturday and Sunday are the weekend. In the Arab World, Friday is the day when people go to the mosque, and the working week begins on Sunday.

Activity 5

spectator sport = a sport which you watch

participation sport = a sport which you play

hybrid = a mixture

martial arts = for example, *judo*, *karate* and *kendo*

aerobic exercise = exercise which makes you use your heart and lungs

sponsor = support with money

tutoring = teaching, usually in small groups

city dwellers = people who live in the city

devote time = to spend time

pastime = leisure activity, hobby

rural people = people who live in the country

recreation = leisure activities

passion = a love

range = variety

enthusiasm = a great interest in something

13 Friends

In this unit we look at how we make friends and what we expect them to do for us, or us for them. We also look at some situations where something has gone wrong between friends.

Activity 1

Remember that *buddy* is an informal word.

Activity 2

In some cultures, it's common to have lots of friends, and different groups of friends, whom you may see regularly, or just occasionally. In other cultures, you may have a small group of friends with whom you spend much of your leisure time. Which is more common in your culture?

Activity 3

Remember: *I lend you something* = I give it you and you give it back later. *I borrow something from you* = you give me something, and I give it back later.

lie = not tell the truth

be available = be ready

Activity 5

settling in = adapting to live somewhere for a long time

avoid = not go near

chatting = talking, usually between friends

Activity 6

generous = willing to give time, money or help

nervous = worried or frightened

tremendous = enormous or great

tricky = difficult

bottom line = the conclusion, once you've discussed a matter

Activity 7

No one will expect you to understand what's happening between friends in every cross-cultural context, but it's important to be aware that behavior in your culture may not be transferable to situations in other cultures or with other individuals.

14 Food and Drink

This unit looks at typical food and drink from different cultures. We talk about traditional dishes, mealtimes, special meals, and table manners.

Activity 1

The description of the ingredients in these dishes does not do justice to the care which goes into their recipes. For example, the Moroccan *tagine* involves lots of spices and a special ceramic dish to cook it in. Making *sushi* is an art form in Japan, and there are many different types to try. The *mezes* from Turkey and the Middle East are a wide variety of little dishes, not just those you see in the photo. *Borscht* is eaten in many countries in Eastern and Central Europe, each with their own additional ingredients and special way of preparing the dish.

Activity 2

The food in this activity are all items which Ben mentions. All of them are very common in the USA, except *caviar*, which he uses as an example of the most special food you can offer a guest. It's definitely not common in the USA!

Activity 3

The answers to these questions will vary from culture to culture, family to family and individual to individual. Like much cultural behavior, eating customs and table manners are based on rules which we don't usually learn, but which we acquire through watching our family and friends.

chopsticks = two thin pieces of wood, china or metal which are used to eat food in countries like Japan, China and Korea.

Activity 4

Many people like to 'graze', which means to eat small amounts of food all the time through the day. For most Americans, it's still typical only to eat three times a day.

chips (US) = crisp pieces of fried potato served cold. (UK *crisps*). *Chips* (UK) = fried potatoes served hot (US *fries*).

messy = something which covers your hands with sauce

barbecue = an outside fire where you can cook hamburgers, steak, spare ribs, etc. It can also mean the style of cooking and a party where everyone eats this kind of food.

Activity 6

raw = uncooked

aristocrat = a member of the highest social class in a country

15 Teachers and Students

This unit looks at the relationship between teachers and students in different cultures, and how effective certain teaching techniques are. It examines the role of the teacher and the degree of respect that students show them.

Activity 1

In many schools in the USA, it's common for students to work in small groups around tables, rather than in lines of desks facing the teacher. This is designed to encourage them to be independent and to use their own resources

Activity 4

cheat = to break the rules in an exam by looking at another student's paper or by using secret reference material

Activity 5

elaborate = to go into detail or develop an idea

teachers who are stricter = teachers who demand more discipline in the class

monopolize = demand the most amount of time

Activity 6

pair work = when two students work together

role-plays = when you work in pairs or groups and act out a situation

Unit Notes

16 Gift-giving

In this unit we talk about the different customs of giving gifts around the world. There are, of course, individual preferences in what gifts you give and receive, but many gift-giving customs, such as when you give a gift, how you give it or when you open it, are based on broader cultural traditions. Once again, you may never be able to learn all the different customs, but it's worth being aware that there may be differences, and being ready to ask what they might be.

Activity 1
Some gifts may not be appropriate in certain cultures. A bottle of perfume might be seen as a gift which indicates romance in certain cultures. It may be inappropriate for a man to offer any gift to a woman, even if she is the wife of a business associate. Wine and whisky are unacceptable gifts in Muslim countries. In China a clock suggests the passing of time, and death, and a handkerchief is a symbol of sadness. Money may be very appropriate to, the bride at a Greek wedding, where the guests pin banknotes onto her dress, but not at a British wedding. A pair of scissors indicates the cutting of a relationship in Japan. Underwear in most countries is usually too intimate as a gift unless it's for someone you know very well.

Activity 2
funeral = the ceremony that takes place after someone has just died

Activity 3
passed away = died

Activity 6
candy (US) = *sweets* (UK)

greedy = wanting more than you need

bride = a woman who is getting married.

groom = the man a bride is marrying.

An *even* number = 2, 4, 6, 8, etc.

An *odd* number = 1, 3, 5, 7, etc.

17 Complaining

This unit looks at how and when we complain about something which we feel is unacceptable. In many cultures, people are reluctant to complain. They may be too embarrassed to say anything, or they may feel that a complaint will make them or the person to whom they're complaining lose face. The purpose of this unit is not to teach you how to complain in English, especially if you're reluctant to complain in your own language. It's designed to help you explore how and when you might complain and to teach you the language of complaining, so that you can recognize it.

Activity 2
registration card = the card you fill in when you check in at a hotel

Activity 4
breaking the speed limit = driving faster than the law allows you to

conductor = the person on an Indian bus who sells you a ticket

Activity 7
If you don't enjoy acting out role-plays, you may like to work in pairs and make a list of situations in which you're prepared to complain. Is it ever with people you know? Or is it only with people you don't know, in service situations such as shopping, buying tickets, or with officials?

19 Going on Vacation

This unit looks at the different places people around the world go to on vacation, and talks about the things they do there. It also encourages us to think about what we like about our home and what we miss when we're away.

Activity 1
Here are some facts about the places in the photos

	Location	Size (square km)	Population (approx)	Capital	Special features
Switzerland	Western Europe	41,000	7 million	Bern	mountains and lakes
The Maldives	islands in the Indian Ocean	298	253,000	Malé	beaches
Thailand	South-East Asia	513,000	60 million	Bangkok	mountains, rainforest, beaches
Hong Kong	South-East Asia; an administrative division of the People's Republic of China	1,092	7 million	Beijing	busy city, sea front; shopping
Scotland	The northern region of the United Kingdom	79,000	512,000	Edinburgh	mountains and lakes, monsters and ghosts

Activity 2
snorkeling = when you swim with your face underwater using a mask to see and a *snorkel* to breathe

Activity 3

destination = a place where people go. If you're going to Thailand, Thailand is your *destination*.

Activity 5

Henryk refers to *Mazury*, the lake district in the north-east of Poland. The school year in Poland is divided into two *semesters*.

Raj refers to a *hill station*, which is a village in the mountains, where it is much cooler than the towns lower down. Mosouri and Kulu Manali are examples of *hill stations*.

Ashura talks about *Disney World*, the theme park near Orlando, Florida.

Tahiti is an island in the Indian Ocean.

20 Shopping

This unit looks at one of the most popular leisure activities in the world – shopping. We talk about where people go shopping, who they buy things for, and what they buy.

Activity 1

mall = a huge shopping area with a variety of different shops under one roof

a *department store* is usually on several floors, and sells all kinds of goods, including clothes, toiletries, furniture, toys and household equipment. Sometimes it may also sell food.

drugstore = a pharmacy, where you can buy medicine and toiletries and sometimes food and drink as well.

jeweler = a store where you buy jewelry, such as rings, necklaces, bracelets and watches

Activity 2

palmtop computer = a small computer which you can hold and use in the palm of your hand

Activity 3

cosmetics = make-up, such as lipstick and eyeliner

key rings = small rings to keep your keys on

souvenirs = things you buy which remind you of a place you've visited.

Activity 4

hang out with friends = to spend time with friends

Activity 6

Adriana says she is *renovating my wardrobe*. This means she's throwing out old clothes and buying new ones.

Henryk talks about *intuition*, which means knowing something instinctively. He thinks women know the right things to buy better than men.

Ashura goes *window shopping*, which means she looks in store windows but doesn't buy anything.

Chutima talks about *material*. Here, this means the cloth she chooses for her suits and dresses.

21 Special Occasions

In this unit we look at special occasions around the world, including family occasions and religious events. We talk about how the occasions are celebrated and compare them with other traditional ceremonies in other cultures.

Activity 1

Adolescence is the period when a child begins the process of becoming an adult. It refers to both physical developments and changes in mood and behavior.

Eid is the Muslim festival to celebrate the end of *Ramadan*, the period of one month, when no one eats or drinks during the day.

Retirement is the time when people stop going to work and use their savings or pension to live on.

Activity 3

Most cultures have a special ceremony to welcome the arrival of a new baby. In some cultures, it may take place within the first few days, in others, it may be a few months or even a year before the celebration takes place.

Different birthdays have different significance. In the West, there may be a special birthday when the child becomes a teenager (13), or when the person has the right to vote (18 or 21).

feast = a large and special meal, often with many dishes

Some people think *evil spirits* make you do bad things.

chant = to sing or to repeat a phrase, especially a religious or political one, as if you were singing

Unit Notes

Raj talks about the *holy scriptures*, which are writings from the most important book of a religion, such as the *Koran* or the *Bible*.

Valentina talks about a *wake*, which is a gathering after a person has died, when friends and relatives eat, drink and share memories of the dead person.

Henryk talks about the fiftieth anniversary as *the golden anniversary*. The twenty-fifth is the *silver anniversary*, the fortieth is the *ruby anniversary*, and the sixtieth is the *diamond anniversary*. All the other wedding anniversaries have similar names. Your *marriage vows* are the promises you make to your partner when you marry.

Chutima mentions the *coffin*, which is the box the body of a dead person is placed in.

incense = something you burn for its pleasant smell during religious ceremonies

temple = a holy place where people pray

monks = holy men

Chutima talks about *turtles*, which are reptiles with a hard shell and which live on land and in the water.

22 Work Customs

This unit examines different work customs around the world. It looks at the kind of benefits workers might expect in different companies or organizations, and encourages you to think about the conditions you would look for in an ideal job.

Activity 1

The two photos draw attention to some of the important differences between working practices in the East and in the West. In the USA, business can appear to be very informal. Employees' desks are likely to be highly personalized, with family photos and reminders of home. Employers and employees are likely to use first names. The higher ranking members of staff like to have an office with a window, and usually leave their doors open to encourage visitors, unless they're in a meeting. But the air of informality is superficial. If an employee misbehaves, the formality of the company situation returns. It's sometimes confusing for visitors who are not aware of this kind of company culture to understand working customs.

Activity 3

bonuses = extra payments which you may receive once or twice a year if you have performed well in your job

retirement fund = money from the state or from a savings plan, often organized by your company which you live on when you have retired

cafeteria = a place where you can buy meals. Sometimes the food has been partly paid for by the employer

company car = a car paid for by the company, but which you can use either for your work or for personal reasons

transport allowance = money which your company gives you to pay for travel between your home and your place of work

Activity 5

qualifications = the exams you passed at school or university, and other diplomas or degrees you have taken during your training

gender = whether you are male or female

ability to cope in a crisis = you can do what's necessary when something serious goes wrong

Activity 6

perks = something you get from your employer in addition to your salary

23 Weddings

This unit looks at traditional weddings around the world, and in particular, in Britain, Thailand and Jordan. All cultures celebrate the marriage of two people, usually in an elaborate ceremony, but it is the details of the different wedding customs which make the topic such an interesting one.

Activity 1

The photo shows a traditional British church wedding. As the text in 2 will explain, many people choose not to marry in church, but this is the most traditional form of the wedding in the UK, and even couples who are not religious often want their wedding day to observe age-old customs.

However, it may be worth pointing out that one in three marriages in Britain ends in divorce, and the Church is usually unwilling to marry couples who have already been divorced.

The *bridegroom* is often referred to as the *groom*.

Activity 2

registry office = a government building where people get married. It is sometimes part of the town hall.

vow = a promise

confetti = small pieces of colored paper, dried flowers or rice, which wedding guests throw over the bride and groom

reception = the party held after the marriage ceremony

Chutima refers to a *loan*, which is something, like money, which someone lends.

sugar cane = the plant which you get sugar from

a *photo album* = a special book where you keep photos

Deema refers to a *hen-night*, which is a party which usually takes place the evening before the wedding with all the bride's female friends.

Appliances or *household appliances* are washing machines, cookers, or food mixers, etc.

 Cultural Identity and Values

This unit looks at the relationship between the individual and the culture or the state they belong to. We have seen that our culture is not just defined by where we live, but also by our individual identity and other factors such as gender, age, and background. However, all these individual aspects contribute to the culture which is shared by many others, and which is reflected in a variety of cultural concepts, values, icons, and symbols. Words and ideas all reflect something of the culture of the person who uses them, and in this unit we find out more about our cultural identity.

Activity 1

Remember that when you discuss the ideas you associate with these words, you probably won't have exactly the same ones. Even if you belong to the same local, regional or national culture, there will always be individual differences.

Activity 2

boarding school = a school where you not only have lessons, but where you also spend the night

priest = a holy man

fundamental = basic

fun = something you enjoy

oppression = an unfair or cruel effect

Activity 4

criminal = someone who does something against the law, such as steal something or kill someone

compensate for deficiencies = to make up for something you don't have

Activity 5

Henryk mentions *destiny*, which is what will happen to you in the future.

Deema talks about *God's will*, which is what God wants to happen.

Activity 6

patriotism = the respect you have for your country

solidarity = the cooperation and support you show for other people, especially those you work with

 Face

This unit explores face, which is your personal reputation or prestige as seen by other people. It's a common value in many cultures, but may show itself in different and sometimes opposing ways. For example, losing your temper may, in certain cultures, show that you're being assertive. In other cultures it shows you're losing control. Saying *I don't know* may show that you're being honest, or that you're ignorant. Telling someone off may show that you're the boss, but it may shame the person you're speaking to.

Activity 4

contradict someone = disagree with someone

show off = try to impress other people

be *modest* = not to have too high an opinion of yourself

be *humiliated* = have damaged pride

weigh a ton = be very heavy

Activity 7

Corruption is when someone is dishonest for their own personal gain.

26 People Like You

This unit looks at how we see other people, and at how other people see us. Particularly when we talk about cultural stereotypes, such as 'the English are cold' or 'the Germans have no sense of humor', we are making generalizations of how we see these cultures. But this may not be an accurate picture, and it may be an entirely different picture which the English and the Germans have of themselves: the English respect other people's privacy, and the Germans have a good sense of humor, it's simply not the same as yours. One of the intentions of this book is to explore these stereotypes about cultures, to examine them to see if they're true and to encourage you not to rely on simplistic generalizations. As such, stereotypes do no harm; in fact, they can give us a useful idea of a culture. But as soon as a stereotype becomes a prejudice ('I hate the English because they're so cold.') we could be close to a situation in which conflict can break out.

Activity 1

The photos are all chosen to illustrate positive, but stereotypical activities in the USA, Britain, Australia and Italy. Which images would show your own country in a positive way? Are there any negative stereotypical images, both for

Unit Notes

the countries in the photos and your own country? Which present a more accurate picture?

If you're *racist*, you don't like people who don't belong to your race.

If you're *ignorant*, you don't have much general knowledge and are not open to new experiences.

Activity 2

The questions focus on your individual and family cultural identity, as well as that of the town, region, or country you come from.

Activity 3

At the end of the activity, ask yourself if there is a difference between how people see you and how you see yourself.

Activity 4

Ben's interview is a good example of the aim of this unit, which is to look at the relationship between how people see themselves, and how others see them. He is aware of how some Americans must appear to people from other cultures, but he is nevertheless proud of his culture's achievements, and is aware of its positive characteristics.

Meetings and Negotiations

In this unit we look at business customs in different countries around the world. We look at a number of critical incidents, situations where something has gone wrong, and we explore the reasons for the mistake or the embarrassment. We also talk about more routine matters of business practice using the phone, running meetings, and discussing non-business matters.

Activity 1

The photos have been chosen to set the scene for the work in this unit. Can you say what kind of business might go on in the offices you see?

Activity 2

negotiate = discuss the terms of agreement when you buy or sell something

client = the person you'd like to sell something to

were *interrupted* = someone caused the meeting to stop in order to discuss another matter

purchase = something you buy

bribe = money given to persuade someone to help you by doing something dishonest

Activity 3

motto = a common phrase or saying

be *disruptive* = interrupt someone or something regularly

Activity 5

This activity describes business situations in which people from different cultures behave in different ways. It shows how, by simply doing what they feel is culturally appropriate, people may sometimes cause their foreign co-workers confusion.

Activity 6

emergency = an urgent situation

deal = an agreement, or a successful negotiation. Sometimes when you finalize a negotiation, you say 'It's a deal!' and shake hands.

chairman = the head of a company

executive = a senior manager in a company

29 Holidays and Festivals

This unit looks at different public holidays and festivals. The calendar shows holidays and festivals in Canada. Because Canada is a dominion of the United Kingdom, there are several public occasions which celebrate the close link between the two countries. Like the USA, Canada also celebrates Thanksgiving, but in October, and not in November.

Activity 1

Christmas = the celebration of the birth of Jesus Christ

The Day of the Dead = All Soul's Day, celebrated on November 2, especially in Mexico

Diwali = the Hindu festival of light, held in the autumn

Easter = the celebration of the death and resurrection of Jesus Christ

Eid = the festival which marks the end of *Ramadan*

Halloween takes place during the evening of the 31 October when children in the USA, Canada and the UK dress up as witches or ghosts and go from door to door asking for candy or playing tricks.

Harvest festival = the celebration in early autumn of the safe collection of the crops

Holy Week = the week which leads up to Easter

May Day takes place on May 1. It's a celebration of the arrival of spring, as well as a festival to celebrate workers around the world.

Remembrance Day = the Sunday nearest to November 11, when the dead of recent wars are remembered.

St Valentine's Day is on February 14, when people send romantic cards to others, often without signing them.

Thanksgiving in the USA is in November and celebrates the first harvest of the Pilgrim Fathers in North America. In Canada it's also a festival of thanks for the harvest, but is held in October.

Activity 3

Raj mentions *charity work*. This means helping people who need food, money, clothes, or other forms of help or care.

Valentina mentions *offerings*, which are gifts to Maria, who was the mother of Jesus. *swear* = to use bad language

Henryk mentions *crops*, which are wheat, oats, barley and other plants which grow in fields and are used for food.

Chutima mentions that Buddha *passed away on this day*. This is the day he died.

 30 Men and Women

In this unit we look at customs and attitudes in the relationship between men and women, both in the work place and at home. It examines the role of women and men in traditional contexts and discusses if and to what extent attitudes have changed in recent years.

Activity 1

The photos have been chosen because they show men and women in common, but not stereotypical jobs. You may wish to discuss with your classmates if women can be good soldiers, for example, or men can be good nurses.

Activity 2

mistress = a women who has a male lover, but who is not married to him. He is usually married to someone else.

allowance = a regular payment of money, often taken from the family budget

Activity 3

co-educational school = a school for boys and girls

nowadays = these days

Activity 5

lonely = feeling alone and without friends

pregnant = expecting a baby

get splashed = when water from the street makes you and your clothes wet

sexist = believing that men and women should be treated in a different way

Activity 7

Raj uses the word *priority*. This means the thing which is most important.

helps = servants

 31 Table Manners

This unit looks at some of the customs and rituals which take place at meals around the world. It looks at what you say when you raise your glass, and at the different stages of a dinner.

Activity 1

toast = the act of raising your glass in honor of someone special or a special occasion

Activity 3

The toastmaster, or *Tamada* comes from the country of Georgia, which is in south-eastern Europe on the border with Asia. When Georgia was a republic of the Soviet Union, it was famous for its fruit, wine, and other produce throughout the USSR. It remains well-known for the quality of its food and for its hospitality.

Activity 7

Ben mentions *dessert*, which is the last course of a meal. It's usually a sweet dish, such as ice-cream, fruit, or cake.

Ashura mentions a *couch*, which is a low seat, perhaps with cushions, with places for two or more people.

32 School

This unit looks at schools around the world. We look at school facilities in different cultures and how the school day is organized. We also find out about the education system in different countries.

Activity 1

The photos have been chosen to draw attention to the very different schools that exist around the world.

Activity 2

sports field = a field which is part of the school and used for soccer, baseball, and other sports

auditorium = where a large number of students will gather to hear notices from the teachers, and take part in other communal activities

cafeteria = a self-service restaurant for meals or snacks

gymnasium = a large hall for physical exercise

vending machine = an automatic machine which sells chocolate, chips, drinks and sandwiches

dormitories = rooms where the students in certain schools, called *boarding schools*, sleep

Activity 4

If something is *compulsory*, it means you have to do it.

compulsory schooling = the period during which you have to go to school

university entrance exam = an exam you have to take to enter university

Unit Notes

Activity 6

Henryk mentions *reform*, which means a reorganization.

a *housing estate* = an area of houses built and owned by the town council, and rented by the inhabitants

obligatory = compulsory

demographic explosion = the strongly growing population

 Homeland

This unit explores our roots and our feelings towards the place where we live. When you ask people where they are from, their answer will depend on who they're talking to, but some will say their home town, some will say their home region, some will say the town where they live, and others will say their country. Your answer gives an indication of the relative importance of these different places in your life.

Activity 1

The photo shows a street scene in London, a city with a *broad ethnic mix*, which means a mixture of people from different countries, cultures, races and religions, and where there is considerable harmony and tolerance between everyone who lives there. In London, and in many other cities, the immigrant population has been established for several generations, and its members have a similar sense of 'belonging' as the original inhabitants.

Activity 2

get in touch = make contact

Activity 4

ethnic = belonging to a particular culture or race

Activity 6

Ashura mentions a *tribe*, which is a very large family of people from the same ethnic background. It's often used to describe large groups of people in, for example, Africa.

Henryk uses the word *assimilated*, which means *become part of*.

34 Ancestors

This unit looks at our attitudes towards old people, especially older members of our own families, and our ancestors. In some cultures, it is more common to remember and respect ones ancestors than in others. It explores the influence that older people may continue to have over younger people, and discusses issues such as who looks after people when they grow old.

Activity 2

candle = something made of wax and when you burn it, it gives off light. You burn it when you go to church when you pray, or to remember your ancestors.

cemetery = a place where a large number of people are buried

grave = the place in the ground where the dead body is

skull = the bone of the head; a symbol of death

hearse = the special car which takes the coffin to the funeral

coffin = the box which the dead body is buried in

Activity 6

Deema refers to a *nursing home*, which is a kind of hospital for elderly people who need help looking after themselves.

James refers to a *tomb*, which is like a grave; a place where a dead person is buried.

Ashura uses the word *wisdom*, which is the knowledge and experience someone has collected during their life.

snake = a long, thin reptile without legs, which slips along the ground. *Python* = a type of snake

 Time

This unit looks at the attitudes of different cultures towards the concept of time. It makes the distinction between clock time and natural time. In our busy lives we are influenced by the clock: it's time to get up and go to school or to work, it's time to catch the train, it's time to have lunch. In the natural world, there's a different form of time. Flowers bloom when they're ready in the spring, trees lose their leaves at some time in the autumn, and people eat when they're hungry, not when the clock tells them to. Many cultures are influenced by both of these contradictory types of time.

Activity 2

specific = particular

punctual = on time. Someone who is punctual does things on time.

Question 9: Remember that summer in the Northern Hemisphere is June 21 to September 20 and summer in the Southern Hemisphere is December 21 to March 20.

Activity 8

A *stitch* is a short length of, for example, cotton which someone has passed through two pieces of material to join them. The proverb means that if something is torn, it's better to mend it quickly than leave it until later, when it may need a lot more work.

Introducing Yourself   1

I'm *(Maria)*.
I'm from *(the USA)*.
I live in *(New York)*.

I'm *(20)* years old.
I'm a *(student)*.

Greetings   2

Formal

Good morning.
Good afternoon.

Good evening.
Good day.

A: How do you do?   B: How do you do?

Informal

Hi!   Hello.
Good day. (Australian English)

Formal or informal

Pleased to meet you.

A: How are you?
B: I'm *(very well / fine thanks)*. And you?

Asking Questions   3

Are you *(Japanese)*?	Yes, I am. / No, I'm not.
Is he *(Korean)*?	Yes, he is. / No, he isn't.
Do you speak *(English)*?	Yes, I do. / No, I don't.
Does she live in *(Taipei)*?	Yes, she does. / No, she doesn't.

What nationality are you?
How do you say *(sayonara)* in English?
Where were you born?

Can I use your *(dictionary)*?
Could I open the window?
Would you mind lending me a *(pen)*?
Could you tell me the time, please?
I wonder if you could help me.

Sounding Fluent   4

I'm sorry, could you repeat that?
I'm sorry, I don't understand.
I'm sorry, I didn't hear that.

Could you speak more slowly?
What does *(given name)* mean?
How do you say *(arigato)* in English?
How do spell *(engineer)*?
How do you pronounce this word?

Showing You're Listening   5

I see.	How interesting!
Uh-huh.	Yes.
Really?	Right.

Talking About Your Customs and Culture   6

In my country, *(women do most of the shopping)*.
Most people *(stay at home until they marry)*.
Some people *(wear traditional clothes)*.
But in my family we *(wear Western-style clothes)*.

We always *(spend Christmas together)*.
We usually *(see the whole family once a month)*.
I often *(go to a soccer game on Sunday)*.
I sometimes *(go out with friends)*.
I hardly ever *(complain in a restaurant)*.
I never *(stay out late during the week)*.

It's the same / similar in my country.
It's different to my country.

Talking About Customs and Rules   7

You have to *(take off your shoes)*.
You shouldn't *(wear a hat)*.
You mustn't *(wear a hat)*. (British English)
You can *(bow or shake hands)*.
You should *(bend your knee and make the sign of the cross)*.

Asking for Permission   8

Is it all right / OK if I *(smoke)*?
Do you mind if I *(open the window)*?

Yes, sure.   Yes, of course.
Not at all. (= I don't mind.)

I'm sorry, but I'd rather you didn't.

Offering   9

Would you like me to *(open the window)*?
Do you want me to do that for you?

Yes, thanks.   No, it's OK, thanks.
That would be great!

Requesting   10

Could you *(turn the music down)*, please?
I wonder if you could *(close the door)*.

Sure.   Of course.
OK.   Right.

I'm afraid …

Chatfile

Complaining 11

Excuse me, but could you *(drive a little more slowly)*.
Please could you *(drive a little more slowly)*?
I'm in a hurry.
I'm afraid my *(soup is cold)*.

Apologizing 12

I'm (very) sorry about that.
I'm sorry *(I'm late)*.
Sorry.
Sorry to bother you, but there's a problem with *(my ticket)*.

Excuse me.	Pardon me.
That's OK.	Don't worry.

Attracting Someone's Attention 13

Polite

Excuse me!	Pardon me!

Informal

Hey!

Talking About Your Feelings 14

I feel angry.	It makes me upset.
I felt upset.	It made me feel happy.

Describing Dishes 15

It's made with *(pork and beans)*.	It's a *(Brazilian)* dish.
It has *(tomatoes and spices)* in it.	It's delicious / very filling.
It takes a long time to cook.	It's called *(feijoada)*.

Giving Advice 16

I think you should *(sit with your friends)*.
If I were you, I'd *(work hard)*.
Make sure you *(do your homework)*.
Don't forget to *(stand up when the teacher comes in)*.

Telling the Time 17

You write	You say
1 o'clock	one o'clock
2.05	five after two
	five past two (British English)
3.10	ten after three
4.15	a quarter after four / four fifteen
5.20	twenty after five / five twenty
6.25	twenty-five after six / six twenty-five
7.30	half past seven (British English)
	seven thirty
8.35	eight thirty-five / twenty-five to nine
9.40	nine forty / twenty to ten
10.45	ten forty-five / a quarter to eleven
11.50	eleven fifty / ten to twelve
12.55	twelve fifty-five / five to one

It's about five thirty.
It's nearly six forty-five.

Times of the Day

morning	until 12 noon
afternoon	until 6 p.m.
evening	until 10 or 11p.m.
night	until 6 a.m.

Talking About Dates 18

You write	You say
2 February	February second *or*
	The second of February
21 June	June twenty-first *or*
	The twenty-first of June

You can write the date in different ways:

day-month-year	10 March 2003
	10/03/03
or month-day-year	March 10 2003
	03/10/03

Years

1845	eighteen forty-five
1972	nineteen seventy-two
2001	two thousand and one
2010	two thousand and ten

Giving Opinions 19

I think that *(most people live in apartments)*.
In my opinion *(stereotypes are not a good thing)*.

Agreeing and Disagreeing 20

Yes, I agree.	That's right.
Well, I'm not sure.	I don't think that's right.

Describing a Picture 21

At the top / bottom ...	In the foreground
On the left / right ...	In the middle
In the background there is a ...	